AFRICAN POLITICAL, ECONOMIC, AND SECURITY ISSUES

LIBYA

LIBERATION AND POST-QADHAFI TRANSITION

African Political, Economic, and Security Issues

Additional books in this series can be found on Nova's website under the Series tab.

Additional E-books in this series can be found on Nova's website under the E-books tab.

Global Political Studies

Additional books in this series can be found on Nova's website under the Series tab.

Additional E-books in this series can be found on Nova's website under the E-books tab.

AFRICAN POLITICAL, ECONOMIC, AND SECURITY ISSUES

LIBYA

LIBERATION AND POST-QADHAFI TRANSITION

BRENTON L. KERR
AND
MEREDITH I. CANTU
EDITORS

Nova Science Publishers, Inc.
New York

Additional color graphics may be available in the e-book version of this book.

Library of Congress Cataloging-in-Publication Data

ISBN 978-1-61942-615-3

Published by Nova Science Publishers, Inc. † New York

CONTENTS

PREFACE

After more than 40 years of authoritarian repression and eight months of armed conflict, fundamental political change has come to Libya. The killing of Muammar al Qadhafi on October 20th and the declaration of Libya's liberation by the interim Transitional National Council on October 23rd marked the end of the Libyan people's armed struggle and the formal beginning of the country's transition to a new political order. This book explores how Libya will face key questions about basic terms for transitional justice, a new constitutional order, political participation, and Libyan foreign policy. Security challenges, significant investment needs, and vigorous political debates are now emerging.

Chapter 1- The uprising in Libya against the government of Muammar al Qadhafi was the subject of evolving domestic and international debate about potential international military intervention, including the proposed establishment of a no-fly zone over Libya. On March 17, 2011, the United Nations Security Council adopted Resolution 1973, establishing a no-fly zone in Libyan airspace, authorizing robust enforcement measures for the arms embargo established by Resolution 1970, and authorizing member states "to take all necessary measures ... to protect civilians and civilian populated areas under threat of attack in the Libyan Arab Jamahiriya, including Benghazi, while excluding a foreign occupation force of any form on any part of Libyan territory."

Chapter 2- After more than 40 years of authoritarian repression and eight months of armed conflict, fundamental political change has come to Libya. The killing of Muammar al Qadhafi on October 20 and the declaration of Libya's liberation by the interim Transitional National Council on October 23 marked the end of the Libyan people's armed struggle and the formal beginning of the country's transition to a new political order. Overcoming the legacy of Qadhafi's rule and the effects of the recent fighting is now the principal challenge for the Libyan people, the TNC, and the international community. The transition period may prove to be as complex and challenging for Libyans and their international counterparts as the recent conflict. Immediate tasks include establishing and maintaining security, preventing criminality and reprisals, restarting Libya's economy, and taking the first steps in a planned transition to democratic governance. In the coming weeks and months, Libyans will face key questions about basic terms for transitional justice, a new constitutional order, political participation, and Libyan foreign policy. Security challenges, significant investment needs, and vigorous political debates are now emerging.

Chapter 3- THE PRESIDENT: Good afternoon, everybody. Today, the government of Libya announced the death of Muammar Qaddafi. This marks the end of a long and painful chapter for the people of Libya, who now have the opportunity to determine their own destiny in a new and democratic Libya.

For four decades, the Qaddafi regime ruled the Libyan people with an iron fist. Basic human rights were denied. Innocent civilians were detained, beaten and killed. And Libya's wealth was squandered. The enormous potential of the Libyan people was held back, and terror was used as a political weapon.

Today, we can definitively say that the Qaddafi regime has come to an end. The last major regime strongholds have fallen. The new government is consolidating the control over the country. And one of the world's longest-serving dictators is no more.

One year ago, the notion of a free Libya seemed impossible. But then the Libyan people rose up and demanded their rights. And when Qaddafi and his forces started going city to city, town by town, to brutalize men, women and children, the world refused to stand idly by.

Chapter 4- Libya has a small population in a large land area. Population density is about 50 persons per sq. km. (80/sq. mi.) in the two northern regions of Tripolitania and Cyrenaica, but falls to less than one person per sq. km. (1.6/sq. mi.) elsewhere. Ninety percent of the people live in less than 10% of the area, primarily along the coast. More than half the population is urban, mostly concentrated in the two largest cities, Tripoli and Benghazi. Thirty-three percent of the population is estimated to be under age 15.

Native Libyans are primarily a mixture of Arabs and Berbers. Small Tebou and Tuareg tribal groups in southern Libya are nomadic or semi-nomadic. Among foreign residents, the largest groups are citizens of other

African nations, including North Africans (primarily Egyptians and Tunisians), West Africans, and other Sub-Saharan Africans.

In: Libya
Editors: B. L. Kerr and M. I. Cantu

ISBN: 978-1-61942-615-3

Chapter 1

OPERATION ODYSSEY DAWN (LIBYA): BACKGROUND AND ISSUES FOR CONGRESS*

Jeremiah Gertler

SUMMARY

The uprising in Libya against the government of Muammar al Qadhafi was the subject of evolving domestic and international debate about potential international military intervention, including the proposed establishment of a no-fly zone over Libya. On March 17, 2011, the United Nations Security Council adopted Resolution 1973, establishing a no-fly zone in Libyan airspace, authorizing robust enforcement measures for the arms embargo established by Resolution 1970, and authorizing member states "to take all necessary measures ... to protect civilians and civilian populated areas under threat of attack in the Libyan Arab Jamahiriya, including Benghazi, while excluding a foreign occupation force of any form on any part of Libyan territory."

In response, the United States established Operation Odyssey Dawn, the U.S. contribution to a multilateral military effort to enforce a no-fly zone and protect civilians in Libya. Military operations under Odyssey Dawn commenced on March 19, 2011. U.S. and coalition forces quickly established command of the air over Libya's major cities, destroying

* This is an edited, reformatted and augmented version of a Congressional Research Service publication, CRS Report for Congress R41725, from www.crs.gov, dated March 28, 2011.

portions of the Libyan air defense network and attacking pro-Qadhafi forces deemed to pose a threat to civilian populations.

From the outset of operations, the Obama administration declared its intent to transfer command of operations over Libya to a coalition entity. On March 28, 2011, the NATO Secretary General announced that NATO would take over command of all aspects of military operations within a few days.

Establishment of the initial no-fly zone over Libya went smoothly. One U.S. aircraft was lost due to mechanical malfunction, but the crew were rescued. Estimates of the cost of the initial operation range between $400 million and $1 billion.

U.S. participation in Operation Odyssey Dawn and NATO operations around Libya raises a number of questions for Congress, including the role of Congress in authorizing the use of force, the costs of the operation, the desired politico-strategic end state, the role of U.S. military forces in an operation under international command, and many others.

(A note on transliteration: The name of Muammar al Qadhafi is transliterated in many ways by various sources. This paper refers to him as Qadhafi except when quoting other documents, wherein his name is represented as it appears in the source.)

Prior to Military Operations: Background, Select Views, and Authorization[1]

In the weeks prior to commencement of Operation Odyssey Dawn, the ongoing uprising in Libya against the government of Muammar al Qadhafi was the subject of domestic and international debate about potential international military intervention, including the proposed establishment of a no-fly zone over Libya. On March 17, 2011, the United Nations Security Council adopted Resolution 1973 (UNSCR 1973), establishing a no-fly zone in Libyan airspace, authorizing robust enforcement measures for the arms embargo established by Resolution 1970, and authorizing member states "to take all necessary measures ... to protect civilians and civilian populated areas under threat of attack in the Libyan Arab Jamahiriya, including Benghazi, while excluding a foreign occupation force of any form on any part of Libyan territory."

Policy debates in the United States, allied countries, and the Middle East have intensified in parallel with the authorization, launch, and continuation of U.S. and coalition military operations. Third parties, including the U.S.

government, have staked out firm political positions demanding Qadhafi's ultimate departure, but opposition forces have yet to demonstrate that they have the capacity to dislodge Qadhafi on their own, and Resolution 1973 calls for an immediate cease-fire and dialogue, which Qadhafi may yet embrace in a bid to stay in power. For the United States, reconciling a long-term objective of regime change with participation in military action to enforce a UN Security Council resolution that does not expressly endorse that goal is a particular challenge. Some observers have warned that the use of force—whether by external parties, Libyan rebels, or some combination of the two—to affect regime change in Tripoli may have unpredictable consequences for the long term stability of the country and the region.

Administration Perspectives

President Obama has stated that the United States believes that Muammar al Qadhafi and his government have lost legitimacy and that Qadhafi should relinquish power and leave the country. The President and his Administration took a number of non-military policy steps to achieve that goal, including supporting U.N. Security Council Resolution 1970, which imposes an international arms embargo on Libya and imposes targeted financial and travel sanctions on Qadhafi, some of his family members, and prominent officials of his government.[2] Prior to the adoption of Resolution 1973, the President and U.S. officials emphasized that "all options" have remained under consideration during the current crisis. Insofar as Resolution 1973 "demands the immediate establishment of a cease-fire," it is unclear whether U.S. action in pursuit of its previously stated goal of securing an end to Qadhafi's rule would be compatible with the authorizations set out in the new Resolution.

Civilian defense officials and uniformed military officers have discussed the political and operational considerations that have shaped the Administration's decision making process with regard to a possible no-fly zone:

- On March 10, 2011, Defense Secretary Gates said, "We are very mindful of opinion in the region, and that's one of the reasons that one of the three central criteria with respect to any action requires strong regional support. I think that a number of [NATO] ministers made clear that we were—we wanted to put ourselves in a position to assist the Arab League, the African Union or the U.N. in this endeavor, and very sensitive to NATO being responsive to those organizations rather than taking an initiative on its own."[3]

- On March 16, U.S. Ambassador to the United Nations Susan Rice indicated publicly for the first time that the Administration supported discussion by the Security Council of further international steps, including a no-fly zone, with regard to the conflict in Libya. She said, "we need to be prepared to contemplate steps that include, but perhaps [should] go beyond, a no-fly zone at this point, as the situation on the ground has evolved, and as a no-fly zone has inherent limitations in terms of protection of civilians at immediate risk."[4]
- On March 17, 2011, Air Force Chief of Staff General Norton Schwartz "said it would take upwards of a week to establish a no-fly zone and would require U.S. forces to first neutralize Libyan ground to air anti-aircraft sites."[5] General Schwartz added that a no-fly zone itself "would not be sufficient" to reverse recent Libyan government gains against the anti-Qadhafi forces.[6]
- On March 17, Ambassador Rice explained the U.S. vote in favor of Resolution 1973 by stating that the Security Council, "has responded to the Libyan people's cry for help. This Council's purpose is clear: to protect innocent civilians."

President Obama's Remarks on U.S. Military Operations

On March 18, President Obama made a statement on U.S. policy in the wake of the passage of U.N. Security Council Resolution 1973.[7] Passages from that statement included:

> The United States, the United Kingdom, France, and Arab states agree that a cease-fire must be implemented immediately. That means all attacks against civilians must stop. Qaddafi must stop his troops from advancing on Benghazi, pull them back from Ajdabiya, Misrata, and Zawiya, and establish water, electricity and gas supplies to all areas. Humanitarian assistance must be allowed to reach the people of Libya.... Let me be clear, these terms are not negotiable. These terms are not subject to negotiation. If Qaddafi does not comply with the resolution, the international community will impose consequences, and the resolution will be enforced through military action.
>
> Our focus has been clear: protecting innocent civilians within Libya, and holding the Qaddafi regime accountable.
>
> Left unchecked, we have every reason to believe that Qaddafi would commit atrocities against his people. Many thousands could die. A humanitarian crisis would ensue. The entire region could be destabilized,

> endangering many of our allies and partners. The calls of the Libyan people for help would go unanswered. The democratic values that we stand for would be overrun. Moreover, the words of the international community would be rendered hollow.
>
> ... the United States is prepared to act as part of an international coalition.... I have directed Secretary Gates and our military to coordinate their planning, and tomorrow Secretary Clinton will travel to Paris for a meeting with our European allies and Arab partners about the enforcement of Resolution 1973. We will provide the unique capabilities that we can bring to bear to stop the violence against civilians, including enabling our European allies and Arab partners to effectively enforce a no fly zone.
>
> The United States is not going to deploy ground troops into Libya. And we are not going to use force to go beyond a well-defined goal—specifically, the protection of civilians in Libya.

On March 21, 2011, President Obama wrote to congressional leaders announcing that U.S. military forces had commenced operations in Libya on March 19 "to prevent a humanitarian catastrophe and address the threat posed to international peace and security by the crisis in Libya" and "for the purposes of preparing a no-fly zone."[8] The President stated that the "strikes will be limited in their nature, duration, and scope" and that "their purpose is to support an international coalition as it takes all necessary measures to enforce the terms of U.N. Security Council Resolution 1973." He added that, "United States military efforts are discrete and focused on employing unique U.S. military capabilities to set the conditions for our European allies and Arab partners to carry out the measures authorized by the U.N. Security Council Resolution." President Obama cited his "constitutional authority to conduct U.S. foreign relations and as Commander in Chief and Chief Executive," and stated he was reporting to Congress "to keep the Congress fully informed, consistent with the War Powers Resolution."

Congressional Perspectives

Some Members of Congress made statements urging the imposition of a no-fly zone in the case of Libya's uprising, while others have expressed doubt about the utility of such an operation or other military intervention and suggested that the Administration should seek congressional authorization for any use of U.S. armed forces with regard to the Libyan conflict.

- On March 15, 2011, Senator John McCain introduced S.Res. 102, which

> calls on the President... to recognize the Libyan Transitional National Council, based in Benghazi but representative of Libyan communities across the country, as the sole legitimate governing authority in Libya; ...to take immediate steps to implement a "no-fly zone" in Libya with international support; and, ...to develop and implement a comprehensive strategy to achieve the stated United States policy objective of Qaddafi leaving power.

- Also on March 15, 2011, Representative Ron Paul and seven co-sponsors introduced H.Con.Res. 31, which "expresses the sense of Congress that the President is required to obtain in advance specific statutory authorization for the use of United States Armed Forces in response to civil unrest in Libya." The resolution specifically notes the possible imposition of a no-fly zone as one of the possible actions that inspired the legislation.
- Senator Richard Lugar released a statement on March 15 that read, "It is doubtful that U.S. interests would be served by imposing a no-fly zone over Libya. If the Obama Administration is contemplating this step, however, it should begin by seeking a declaration of war against Libya that would allow for a full Congressional debate on the issue."
- On March 16, Senator John Kerry said,

> The international community cannot simply watch from the sidelines as this quest for democracy is met with violence. The Arab League's call for a UN no-fly zone over Libya is an unprecedented signal that the old rules of impunity for autocratic leaders no longer stand. Time is running out for the Libyan people. The world needs to respond immediately to avert a humanitarian disaster. The Security Council should act now to heed the Arab League's call. (see "International Involvement" below)

- Debate within the Senate Foreign Relations Committee at a March 17 hearing on the Middle East revealed differences of opinion among committee members and between some Senators and the Administration with regard to the imperative to intervene; the likely benefits and drawbacks of intervention, including through the establishment of a no-fly zone; the need for congressional authorization for the use of U.S. military forces; and the likelihood that Al Qaeda or other violent Islamists could take advantage of the current situation or future unrest to threaten Libyan and international security.

International Involvement

United Nations Authorization

United Nations Security Council Resolution 1970, adopted on February 26, 2011, did not authorize the use of force by member states with regard to the conflict in Libya or the enforcement of the arms embargo established by the resolution. As such, debate from February 26 through March 17 focused on the need for military intervention and the potential for further authorization from the Security Council.

The no-fly zone provisions of UNSCR 1973 ban "all flights in the airspace of the Libyan Arab Jamahiriya in order to help protect civilians" with the exception of humanitarian flights, evacuation flights, flights authorized for the protection of civilians, and "other flights which are deemed necessary by States acting under the authorization ...to be for the benefit of the Libyan people." Member states are authorized to act nationally or "through regional organizations." All authorized flights are to be coordinated with the U.N. Secretary General and the Arab League Secretary General. The resolution calls on member states "to provide assistance, including any necessary over-flight approvals, for the purposes of implementing" the no-fly zone and civilian protection operations.

It was not clear what immediate steps the United States or others were prepared to take to enforce the no-fly zone or civilian protection provisions of resolution 1973, amid claims from Qadhafi and Libyan opposition figures that the confrontation in and around Benghazi could be reaching a decisive point. Libyan officials replied to the Security Council action by stating, "Any foreign military act against Libya will expose all air and maritime traffic in the Mediterranean Sea to danger and civilian and military [facilities] will become targets of Libya's counter-attack."[9] Libya's reported acceptance of a ceasefire on the morning of March 18 may complicate the decisions of third parties, including the United States, about how to proceed with authorized intervention in general, and a no-fly zone in particular.

Other Organizations and Governments

The adoption of the resolution by the Security Council followed a flurry of international activity and diplomacy addressing the subject of potential military intervention generally and a no-fly zone specifically. On March 12, 2011, the Council of the League of Arab States met to discuss the situation in Libya and endorsed on a consensus basis a request to the U.N. Security Council:

> to take measures to impose a no-fly zone over the movement of Libyan military planes immediately, and to establish safe areas in the places exposed to shelling as preventive measures allowing to provide protection for the Libyan people and the residents in Libya from different nationalities, taking into account the regional sovereignty and integrity of neighboring countries.[10]

The Arab League statement was welcomed by international observers who view regional support as a prerequisite for any direct intervention, including any multilateral military operation to impose a no-fly zone. The U.S. government referred to the decision as "important." Some observers in the region who had expressed concern that third parties, including the United States, had not provided sufficient support to the Libyan opposition strongly supported the Arab League statement. Other observers cautioned that the apparent consensus at the Arab League meeting may have masked underlying dissension among regional governments with regard to specific types of military intervention and strong opposition to any foreign military intervention among some regional citizens.[11]

Those concerns appeared to be borne out when coalition military strikes against Libyan ground forces drew criticism from some Arab leaders after the start of operations on March 19, 2011. On March 21, Arab League Secretary General Amr Moussa said that, from the Arab League's perspective, the purpose of military operations and Resolution 1973 is "not to give the rebels support. It is not a question of supporting a regime, a government or a council."[12] He predicted that if Muammar al Qadhafi remains in control of some or all of Libya then the result could be "a prolonged case of civil war and tension and destruction of Libya." Popular reactions to the Security Council resolution and military operations in different countries vary, and popular views and government positions could shift dramatically depending on the scope, course, and outcome of the military intervention.

Resolution 1973 recognizes "the important role of the League of Arab States in matters relating to the maintenance of international peace and security in the region," and requests that the member states of the Arab League "cooperate with other Member States in the implementation of" measures taken pursuant to the resolution to protect Libyan civilians. The Obama

Administration is seeking "active Arab partnership, both in the measures that would be taken but also in the financial support for them."[13]

For several weeks prior to the beginning of Operation Odyssey Dawn, the North Atlantic Treaty Organization (NATO) monitored Libyan air traffic using AWACS aircraft and assets deployed as part of NATO's Operation Active Endeavor, NATO's longstanding counterterrorism and maritime security operation in the Mediterranean Sea. On March 7, 2011, NATO representatives agreed to increase air surveillance of Libyan air traffic to 24-hours per day. NATO Secretary General Anders Fogh Rasmussen stated, "as a defense alliance and a security organization, it is our job to conduct prudent planning for any eventuality."[14] On March 10, NATO Defense Ministers convened for a previously planned ministerial meeting and discussed the situation in Libya. Following the meeting, NATO announced that it had decided to "increase the presence of NATO maritime assets in the Central Mediterranean," and to begin planning for support of humanitarian operations and more active enforcement of the arms embargo, in anticipation of potential further U.N. Security Council instructions. Secretary General Rasmussen stated that "demonstrable need, a clear legal mandate and solid support from the region," would be the critical factors in determining the scope of further NATO action.

In spite of statements underscoring NATO unity on steps announced to date, there did not appear to be full consensus with the alliance about specific options, including military intervention in the form of a no-fly zone. German officials rejected the use of NATO as a vehicle for organizing the imposition of a no-fly zone or other direct military intervention.[15] Turkish officials initially rejected military intervention and have since agreed to contribute naval forces to participate in NATO Operation Unified Protector to enforce the UN authorized arms embargo on Libya.[16]

France reportedly had resisted NATO command but encouraged NATO to contribute assets for operational coordination. Debate continued over potential NATO command arrangements for coalition military forces through the weekend of March 26.

On March 27, 2011, Secretary General Rasmussen announced that "NATO Allies have decided to take on the whole military operation in Libya under the United Nations Security Council Resolution. Our goal is to protect civilians and civilian-populated areas under threat of attack from the Gaddafi regime. NATO will implement all aspects of the UN Resolution. Nothing more, nothing less."

Details on NATO nations' participation in operations related to Libya follows in "Involvement of Other NATO Member States" below.

MILITARY OPERATIONS[17]

Following passage of UNSCR 1973, on March 19, 2011, U.S. and allied forces established an initial no-fly zone over major cities and air bases near the Libyan coast, as shown in Figure 1. The first offensive operations were carried out by French aircraft striking armored units near Benghazi (see more detail under "France—*Operation Harmattan*" below.)

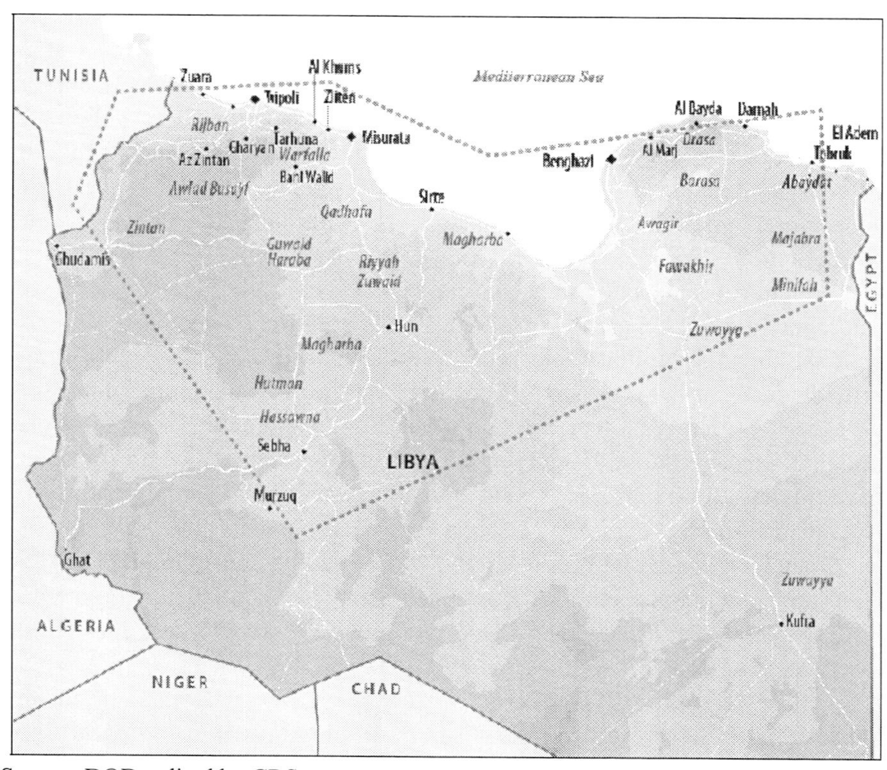

Source: DOD, edited by CRS.
Notes: Locations are approximate.

Figure 1. Initial No-Fly Zone, As of March 19, 2011.

The no-fly operation was enabled by a strike against Libyan air-defense assets and other targets using 110 Tomahawk and Tactical Tomahawk cruise missiles and strikes by three B-2 Spirit bombers delivering 45 Joint Direct Attack Munitions (JDAMs) against Libyan air bases. [18] Tomahawks were also fired from British ships in the area, and British Tornado GR4 aircraft flying from the Royal Air Force base at Marham, England, reportedly employed Storm Shadow cruise missiles.[19]

By March 23, 2011, the no-fly zone had expanded to cover the entire Libyan coastline "boundary to boundary," including Tripoli, and offensive operations were under way against Libyan ground forces observed to pose a threat to civilian populations. However, there was "no indication that Qadafi's forces are pulling back from Misrata or Ajdabiya." [20]

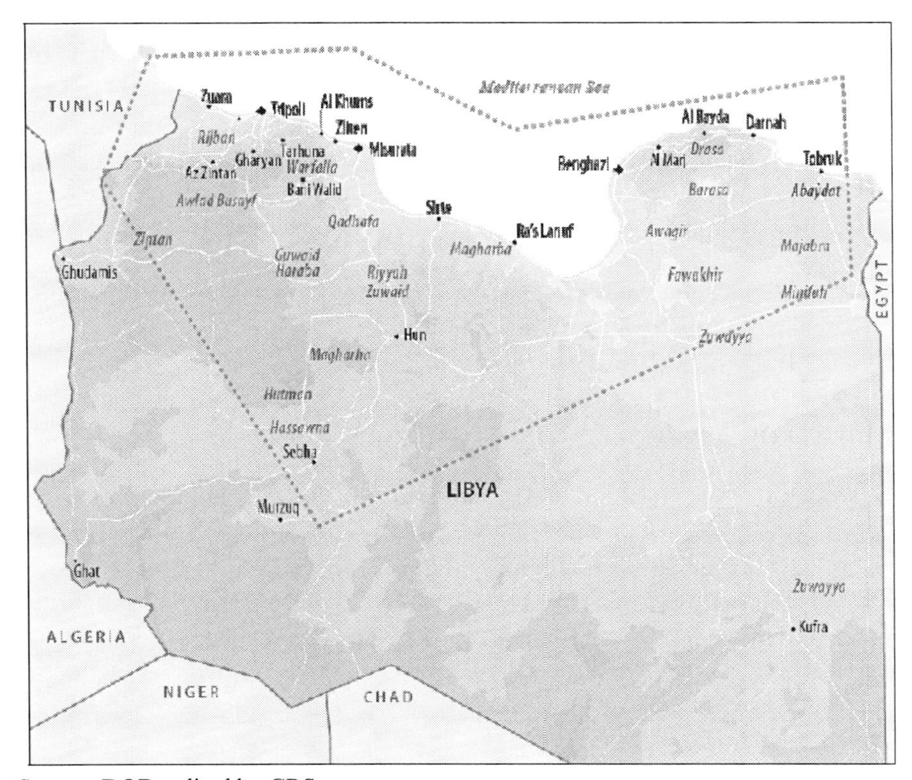

Source: DOD, edited by CRS.
Notes: Locations are approximate.

Figure 2. Expanded No-Fly Zone, As of March 24, 2011.

Operational considerations influencing the scope of Operation Odyssey Dawn include:

Libyan Air Defenses

Gen. James Mattis, Commander, U.S. Central Command, has said:

> You would have to remove the air defense capability, in order to establish the no-fly zone. So it—no illusions here, it would be a military operation. It wouldn't simply be telling people not to fly airplanes.[21]

Libya's air defense system relies on Soviet and Russian systems, most 20-30 years old and at least two generations behind current surface-to-air missile (SAM) technology. Defenses are reportedly focused on Libya's seacoast, which also covers the capital, Tripoli; Benghazi; and Libya's major oil ports.[22] Although it is possible to observe the disposition of radars and missile sites, the condition and effectiveness of the communications, command and control network linking those sites is more difficult to determine.[23] Also, some of the SAM sites are in areas now controlled by the anti-Qadhafi forces, and may not be available to the government.

As of March 22, coalition operations had "rendered Gadhafi's long-range air defenses and his air force largely ineffective."[24]

Libyan Air Assets

The Chief of Staff of the U.S. Air Force estimates that prior to the initiation of Operation Odyssey Dawn, the Libyan air force possessed "multiple tens of combat aircraft," flying only "tens of sorties a day."[25] Although Libya's 10 major air bases notionally house about 180 fighter and attack aircraft and just over 100 helicopters,[26] most are believed inoperable. As Libyan pilots are believed to average only 85 flight hours per year, about half the flight time of coalition air forces, even those aircraft which are operational may not be flown effectively. [27] Libya's aircraft are also rather antiquated, mostly Soviet-era fighters with a few more modern French Mirage jets. On February 21, 2011, two Libyan Air Force colonels flew two of the Mirages to Malta, where they were interned.[28]

As of March 23, 2011, Libya's air force remained grounded. A DOD briefer stated that there had been "no confirmed flight activity by regime forces over the last 24 hours." [29] On March 24, one Libyan jet reportedly flew a mission near Misrata, but was destroyed upon landing by a French fighter.[30] No further Libyan air operations were reported through March 27.

Geography

As noted, most of Libya's major urban centers, as well as its air defense assets, are located along the Mediterranean coast. This has allowed carrier-based and other naval forces to operate in establishing and enforcing a no-fly zone. The four main Libyan air bases are also located near the coast. [31]

Libya borders on Chad, Sudan, Niger, Tunisia, Algeria, and Egypt. However, the most compatible sites to base U.S. forces are across the Mediterranean—Sigonella, Sicily and Souda Bay, Crete. The United States has operated from both bases in the past, and maintains a presence at Sigonella.

> Italy also has cleared partners to base their assets at a variety of facilities, including Gioia del Colle and Amendola in Puglia, Aviano in northeastern Italy, Trapani and Sigonella in Sicily, and Decimomannu in Sardinia. Other bases could be used as many additional allied aircraft are reaching Italy. The NATO CAOC in Poggio Renatico is also fully operational, with other C4I installations heavily involved.[32]

Concept of Operations

As implemented, operations in Operation Odyssey Dawn included strikes on "mechanized forces, artillery...those mobile surface-to-air missile sites, interdicting their lines of communications which supply their beans and their bullets, their command and control and any opportunities for sustainment of that activity" when forces were "attacking civilian populations and cities." [33]

In testimony before the House Armed Services Committee, Marine Corps Commandant General James F. Amos recently called Libya's helicopter forces the "greatest threat" to anti-Qadhafi forces.[34] This would suggest that simply enforcing caps over the main Libyan air bases to suppress fixed-wing flights would not be sufficient to eliminate the main Libyan air threat, and could require operations throughout Libya's airspace. As previously noted, this would be a more complex operation than simply monitoring fixed air bases.

Paragraph 11 of Resolution 1973 "decides that the Member States concerned shall inform the Secretary-General and the Secretary-General of the League of Arab States immediately of measures taken in exercise of the [no-fly zone] authority...including to supply a concept of operations."

U.S. Assets Involved in Operation Odyssey Dawn

U.S. Air Force units participating in Operation Odyssey Dawn include:[35]

- B-2 stealth bombers from the 509th Bomb Wing at Whiteman Air Force Base, MO
- F-15Es from the 492nd Fighter Squadron and 494th Fighter Squadron at RAF Lakenheath, Britain
- F-16CJ defense-suppression aircraft from the 480th Fighter Squadron at Spangdahlem Air Base, Germany
- EC-130 Commando Solo psychological operations aircraft from the 193rd Special Operations Wing, Pennsylvania Air National Guard, Middletown, PA
- KC-135s of the 100th Air Refueling Wing at RAF Mildenhall, Britain and the 92nd Air Refueling Wing, Fairchild AFB, WA
- C-130Js from the 37th Airlift Squadron at Ramstein Air Base, Germany
- A-10 attack fighters
- AC-130 gunships

As part of a 25-hour round trip mission, the B-2s struck combat aircraft shelters at Ghardabiya Airfield in the opening hours of Operation Odyssey Dawn. The F-15Es and F-16CJs attacked ground forces loyal to Qadhafi that were advancing on opposition forces in Benghazi and threatening civilians. KC-135s refueled the strike aircraft en route to an unnamed forward air base, and the C-130Js moved ground equipment and personnel to that forward base, as did theater-based C-17s.[36]

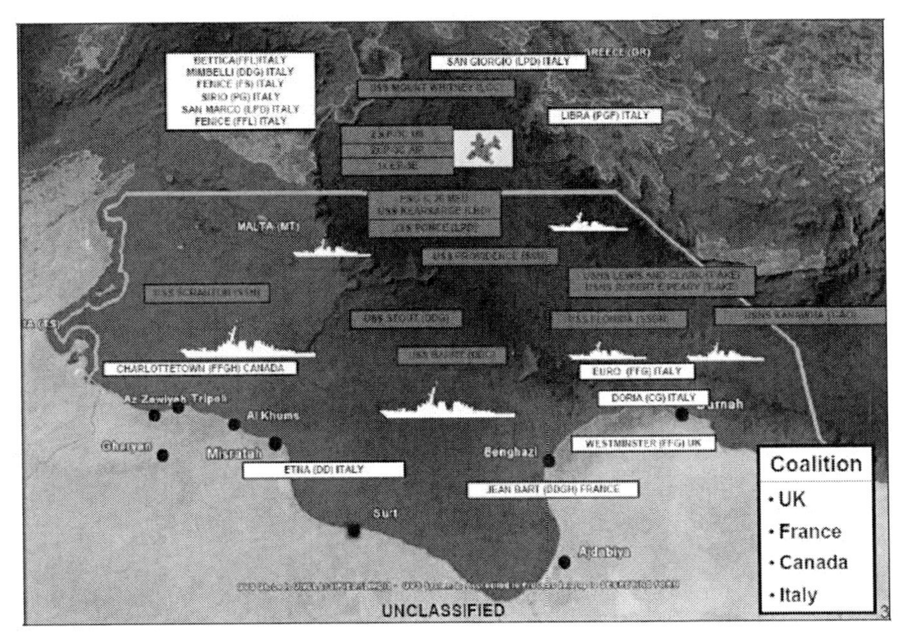

Source: DOD.

Figure 3. Maritime Assets in Operation Odyssey Dawn, As of initiation of operations, March 19, 2011.

U.S. Navy ships involved in Operation Odyssey Dawn include: [37]

- Arleigh Burke-class guided-missile destroyers USS Stout (DDG 55) and USS Barry (DDG 52)
- Submarines USS Providence (SSN 719), USS Scranton (SSN 756) and USS Florida (SSGN 728)
- Marine amphibious ships USS Kearsarge (LHD 3) and USS Ponce (LPD 15)
- Command ship USS Mount Whitney (LCC/JCC 20)
- Support ships Lewis and Clark, Robert E. Peary and Kanawha.

Naval and Marine aviation assets include:

- AV-8B Harrier fighters, CH-53 Super Stallion helicopters and MV-22 Osprey tiltrotor aircraft aboard the Kearsarge and Ponce[38]
- KC-130J tanker aircraft flying from Sigonella Air Base, Italy[39]

- EA-18G Growler electronic attack aircraft of VAQ-132, based at Whidbey Island, WA and flying from Aviano Air Base, Italy. These aircraft were diverted from Iraq to support Operation Odyssey Dawn.[40]
- P-3 Orion sub-hunters and EP-3 Aries electronic attack aircraft[41]

Coalition Forces Involved in Libyan Operations

Coalition air forces include: [42]

- NATO: At least 2 E-3 Sentry AWACS
- United Kingdom: Typhoon and Tornado strike aircraft operating from Gioia del Colle air base in southern Italy; E-3D Sentry, Sentinel and Tristar surveillance aircraft and VC-10 aerial tankers
- France: 20 fighters, including Rafales and Super Etendards from the aircraft carrier Charles de Gaulle. France is also operating land-based Rafales and Mirage 2000s.
- Spain: Four EF-18s operating from Decimomannu air base on Sardinia, a CN235 reconnaissance aircraft, and a tanker
- Denmark: Six F-16s and a transport, operating from Sigonella on Sicily
- Norway: Six F-16s
- Canada: Six CF-18s and two CC-150 refueling tankers
- Belgium: Six F-16s
- Italy: 4 Tornados
- Netherlands: Six F-16s and a KDC-10 tanker
- United Arab Emirates: Six F-16s and six Mirage 2000s
- 12 Qatari fighters arrived March 25

Coalition naval forces include: [43]

- France: Carrier Charles De Gaulle, destroyers Jean Bart, Dupleix, and Forbin, frigate Aconit, oiler La Meuse, and an unnamed nuclear attack submarine.
- Italy: Aircraft carrier Garibaldi, destroyers Andrea Doria and Francesco Mimbelli, frigates Euro and Fenice, support ship Etna,

patrol ships Libra and Sirio, and amphibious ships San Giorgio and San Marco.

- Canada: Frigate Charlottetown
- United Kingdom: Frigates Westminster and Cumberland, submarine Triumph
- Netherlands: One mine-hunter

COMMAND STRUCTURE

The United States took initial operational command of coalition operations to enforce United Nations Security Council Resolution (UNSCR) 1973, with the goal of subsequently transitioning leadership to a coalition commander.[44]

Army General Carter F. Ham, who assumed command of U.S. Africa Command (AFRICOM) on March 9, served as theater commander for the operation.

Tactical operations were coordinated by a Joint Task Force under Admiral Samuel J. Locklear III onboard the command and control ship USS Mount Whitney. Locklear serves jointly as Commander of U.S. Naval Forces Europe and Africa, and as Commander of Allied Joint Force Command, Naples, which has operational responsibility for NATO missions in the Mediterranean. UK and French naval officers are onboard the Mount Whitney, as well as liaison officers from a number of other countries.[46]

Air Force Maj. Gen. Margaret Woodward, commander of 17th Air Force, was the initial Joint Force Air Component Commander for Operation Odyssey Dawn.

Ham

Locklear

Woodward

Figure 4. U.S. Commanders.

The coalition currently includes forces from 13 nations either already in the region or en route. As of March 24, 2011, non-U.S. coalition aircraft were flying "roughly half" of all sorties, up from 13% on March 20.[47,48]

On March 25, 2011, DOD announced that the arms embargo operations had been assumed by NATO on March 23, and that command of the no-fly zone operations had been transferred to NATO on the evening of March 24. [49] NATO announced that it was assuming control of all remaining Libyan operations "with immediate effect" on March 27, 2011.[50] Canadian Lieutenant General Charles Bouchard will command NATO's Libya effort, reporting to Admiral Locklear.[51]

U.S. Africa Command[45]

The U.S. military's newest combatant command, U.S. Africa Command (AFRICOM), which reached full operational capability in October 2008, has taken the lead on Operation Odyssey Dawn.

AFRICOM has also supported the U.S. response to the evolving humanitarian emergency in Libya through the delivery of relief supplies and evacuation of foreign nationals fleeing the violence into neighboring Tunisia.

As envisioned by the Department of Defense (DOD), AFRICOM aims to promote U.S. strategic objectives by working with African states and regional organizations to help strengthen regional stability and security through improved security capability and military professionalization. If directed by national command authorities, its military operations would aim to deter aggression and respond to crises. In March 2011, AFRICOM commenced Operation Odyssey Dawn to protect civilians in Libya as part of a multinational military operation authorized by the U.N. Security Council under Resolution 1973.

Although the precise wording of AFRICOM's mission statement has evolved since the command was first announced, DOD officials have broadly suggested that the command's mission is to promote U.S. strategic objectives by working with African partners to help strengthen stability and security in the region through improved security capability and military professionalization. A key aspect of the command's mission is its supporting role to other agencies and departments efforts on the continent. But like other combatant commands, AFRICOM is expected to oversee military operations, when directed, to deter aggression and respond to crises.

INVOLVEMENT OF OTHER NATO MEMBER STATES[52]

In addition to the United States, at least nine NATO allies have deployed military assets to enforce UNSCR 1973.[53] On the evening of March 27, after a week of coalition air operations under U.S. command, NATO Secretary General Anders Fogh Rasmussen announced that the alliance's 28-member states had directed NATO to take over command and control of the ongoing military operations.[54] The new NATO mission, Operation Unified Protector (OUP), is tasked with enforcing the UN-mandated arms embargo, enforcing a no-fly zone over Libyan air space, and protecting civilians and civilian population areas from being attacked by military forces loyal to the Qadhafi regime. The mission is under the command of Canadian Air Force Lt.Gen Charles Bouchard, headquartered at Allied Joint Force Command in Naples, Italy.

France and the United Kingdom (UK) have been the most vocal proponents of taking action against Qadhafi to protect civilians in Libya—the two countries sponsored UNSC Resolutions 1970 and 1973, and pushed the European Union to quickly adopt sanctions against the Qadhafi regime. They have also played a central role in the ongoing military operations in Libya. Within a week after passage of UNSCR 1970, both French President Nicolas Sarkozy and British Prime Minister David Cameron had publicly called on Qadhafi to relinquish power and each had instructed their respective military leadership to begin working with allies on plans for a no-fly zone over Libya.[55] On March 10, France became the first and only country to recognize the Libyan Transitional National Council "as the legitimate representative of the Libyan people."[56]

On Saturday, March 19, two days after passage of UNSCR 1973, President Sarkozy convened an emergency meeting of allied and Arab leaders in Paris which endorsed the immediate deployment of military aircraft to stop an assault by Qadhafi forces on Benghazi and the establishment of a no-fly zone in the country.[57] Before the end of the meeting, French fighter planes had attacked armored vehicles and tanks belonging to Qadhafi forces on the outskirts of Benghazi. Some participants at the Paris meeting were reportedly critical of the French government both for insisting on convening the meeting before agreeing to endorse air strikes and for then launching strikes before the meeting was over.[58] French officials claim that meeting participants were informed of the operation and argue that the assaults were necessary to prevent an imminent attack on Benghazi. In any case, the strikes had clearly been planned and coordinated with the knowledge of key allied militaries, including the United States and UK. French officials add that the meeting was essential to maintaining coalition unity and Arab League support for military operations and for securing the participation of some Arab governments in the enforcement of UNSCR 1973.

Although U.S. and European forces appear to have met their military objectives during the first week of operations, the planning and initial operational phases were also marked by significant levels of discord within Europe and NATO on the aims and future direction of the mission. Among other things, divergent views within the alliance delayed the swift and clear transfer of command and control responsibilities from the United States to NATO, as proposed by the United States, UK, and other allies. A key point of contention was reportedly the amount of flexibility that NATO forces would be granted to protect civilians and civilian areas, as called for in paragraph 4 of UNSCR 1973. Reports indicate that France insisted on maintaining the ability to target any ground forces that threatened civilian areas, while Turkey reportedly opposed any targeting of ground forces.[59] Adding to the strain within NATO, Germany, the EU's largest and wealthiest member state and a current member of the UN Security Council, abstained from UNSCR 1973 and, opposed to any potential combat operation, on March 23, withdrew its naval assets in the Mediterranean from NATO command.[60] Throughout the first week of operations, other European allies contributing to the mission, including Italy and Norway, expressed increasing frustration with the lack of agreement within NATO, with Norway refusing to deploy its fighter jets unless under they were under NATO command and control.

Only the United States and NATO possess the command and control capabilities necessary for coalition operations enforcing the no-fly zone over Libya and protecting civilians on the ground.

France, along with other allies, has expressed concern that a NATO-led mission in Libya could lead to heightened criticism of western motives in the region. Among other things, they have argued that skepticism of U.S. motives and public perception of NATO as a U.S.-dominated alliance could erode support for the mission within Arab countries. Accordingly, French officials have consistently emphasized the importance of maintaining Arab endorsement of, and involvement in, the ongoing military operations. They have proposed establishing a contact group of nations involved in enforcing UNSCR 1973 that would provide political guidance to NATO and coalition military commanders. An initial meeting of the contact group is set to take place in London on March 29. Media reports indicate that the conference is expected to consist of two meetings—one a council of all governments involved in ongoing military operations, and the other a broader meeting including other Arab and African countries to discuss Libya's future. However, no formal agreement has been reached on how or if a contact group would oversee military operations.

France—Operation Harmattan[61]

In conjunction with U.S. Operation Odyssey Dawn and British Operation Ellamy (discussed below), French military operations against Qadhafi's forces were launched on March 19 under the codename Operation Harmattan. French fighter jets have been heavily involved both in establishing and maintaining a no-fly zone over Libyan territory and in attacking Qaddafi ground forces. France began the allied operations on the morning of March 19, with the aforementioned attack on armored vehicles and tanks on the outskirts of Benghazi. According to the French Ministry of Defense, during each of the first three days of operations approximately 20 French fighter jets were deployed in Libyan airspace, conducting more than 55 sorties, during which five armored vehicles were "neutralized."[62] After initially focusing operations in coastal areas of eastern Libya, on March 24 French planes reportedly hit a Libyan air base about 250 kilometers (155 miles) south of the Libyan coastline. Also on March 24, an air-to-ground missile fired from a French Rafale fighter jet is reported to have hit a Libyan plane that had just landed in the western city of Misrata. The plane had reportedly been flying in breach of the no-fly-zone. French officials report that their fighters are now flying between 150 and 200 sorties each day.

French military assets deployed in the theater of operations consist primarily of approximately 20 combat aircraft—Rafale and Mirage fighter planes—operating out of Solenzara, Corsica, and the aircraft carrier Charles de Gaulle, which carries an additional 26 aircraft, including 16 fighter jets. Along with the Charles de Gaulle, at least four French frigates are reportedly present off the Libyan coast.

President Sarkozy has made a concerted effort to play a leading role both in ongoing military operations in Libya and in the continuing political deliberations about the future of the mission. As mentioned, France was the first—and remains the only—country to afford diplomatic recognition to the Libyan Transitional National Council, Paris hosted the first international conference on Libya's future, and French fighter jets were the first to launch attacks on Libyan ground forces. Sarkozy, whose popularity at home has reached a low-point in recent months, appears to enjoy the support of a wide majority of the French public for his handling of the situation in Libya.[63]

United Kingdom—Operation Ellamy[64]

British military operations against Qadhafi's forces were launched on March 19 under the codename Operation Ellamy. The Royal Navy submarine HMS Triumph participated in the first wave of missile launches against Libyan targets, and reportedly fired approximately 12 Tomahawks in the first three days of the operation. A contingent of Tornado GR4 attack aircraft based in eastern England also took part in the first stages of the assault, making a roundtrip of more than 3,000 miles on March 19-20 to strike targets in Libya. A second long-range Tornado mission, reportedly targeting Qadhafi's presidential compound on the night of March 20, was aborted after late reports of civilians in the target area.

UK airpower deployed in the theatre of operations now consists of two main groups. A detachment of ten Eurofighter Typhoons and a number of Tornados have reportedly deployed to Italy's Gioia del Colle air base, forming the 906 Expeditionary Air Wing. The Typhoons' participation in patrolling and enforcing the no-fly zone marks the aircraft's first ever combat missions. Supporting these combat aircraft is the 907 Expeditionary Air Wing, based at RAF Akrotiri airbase on Cyprus, reportedly consisting of VC-10 tanker aircraft, Nimrod and Sentinel surveillance and reconnaissance planes, E-3D AWACS, and C-17 and C-130 transports. In addition to the Royal Navy submarine, two UK frigates (HMS Cumberland and HMS Westminster) are also present in the Mediterranean waters off the coast of Libya.[65]

A motion in the British parliament's House of Commons supporting the government's action with regard to Libya passed by the overwhelming margin of 557 to 13 on March 21. With approximately 10,000 British troops already deployed in operations in Afghanistan, however, Members of Parliament have expressed serious concerns about the potential scope and duration of this new commitment. As the UK government continues to implement budgetary austerity in order to reduce its budget deficit, there are also concerns about the cost of the Libya operation.

The Daily Telegraph reported that the first four days of Operation Ellamy cost £28.5 million (approximately $45.5 million).[66] Chancellor George

Osborne has stated that the government plans to pay for the operation out of treasury reserves, rather than the main defense budget.

Other Participating NATO Member States

While the U.S., French, and UK militaries have had the clear lead in conducting military operations in Libya thus far, a number of other NATO member states have also begun to participate in the mission.

Italy has provided seven of its airbases for the use of coalition aircraft conducting operations in Libya, and eight Italian combat aircraft (four Tornados and four F-16s) have participated in enforcing the no-fly zone.[67] Libya is a former Italian colony, and the two countries have maintained extensive economic and political ties. In addition, Italy has had serious concerns about a potential influx of large numbers of refugees fleeing instability in Libya and other North African countries. Italy was initially reluctant to take action against Qadhafi's forces—on the third day of operations, Foreign Minister Franco Frattini asserted that "It shouldn't be a war on Libya," that operations must not go beyond implementing UNSCR 1973, and that the coordination should be transferred to NATO as soon as possible.[68]

Canada has committed six CF-18s to help enforce the no-fly zone, as well as two tanker aircraft, two reconnaissance aircraft, and a frigate. The Canadian F-18s reportedly conducted an airstrike on a target near Misrata on March 22.[69] Spain has deployed four F-18s to enforce the no-fly zone and reportedly has one frigate and a submarine in the area of operations. Belgium and Denmark have each committed six F-16s, which have begun taking part in enforcing the no-fly zone.[70] Norway has also deployed six F-16s but has held them on Crete pending clarification of the mission chain of command and rules of engagement.[71] Luxembourg and (non-NATO member) Sweden have reportedly indicated they might commit forces under a NATO umbrella.

Enforcing the Arms Embargo

On March 23, NATO launched a new maritime operation to enforce the arms embargo against the Libyan regime. Naval vessels and aircraft participating in Operation Unified Protector are charged with monitoring the Central Mediterranean off the coast of Libya and, if necessary, intercepting and diverting any vessels suspected of carrying illegal arms or mercenaries in violation of the arms embargo. As a last resort, NATO vessels are empowered to use force in fulfilling their mission. NATO assets will not enter Libyan territorial waters. NATO officials report that as of March 24, ten allies (Belgium, Canada, Denmark, Greece, Italy, the Netherlands, Spain, Turkey, the UK, and the United States) had pledged more than 25 ships and submarines and over 50 fighter jets and surveillance planes to enforce the arms embargo.[72] The Operation will be commanded by Italian Vice Admiral Rinaldo Veri, Commander of Maritime Command Naples.

Issues for Congress

What Is the Role of Congressional Authorization?[73]

Some comments from Members of Congress regarding Operation Odyssey Dawn have addressed the question of congressional authorization—whether and when there is a need for congressional approval based on the War Powers Resolution for a no-fly zone or other operations in and around Libya. The question of whether and how congressional authorization is sought for a proposed operation could have an impact on congressional support—including policy, funding, and outreach to the American people—for the operation.

On November 7, 1973, Congress passed the War Powers Resolution, P.L. 93-148, over the veto of President Nixon. The War Powers Resolution (WPR) states that the President's powers as Commander in Chief to introduce U.S. forces into hostilities or imminent hostilities can only be exercised pursuant to (1) a declaration of war; (2) specific statutory authorization; or (3) a national emergency created by an attack on the United States or its forces. It requires the President in every possible instance to consult with Congress before introducing American armed forces into hostilities or imminent hostilities unless there has been a declaration of war or other specific congressional authorization. It also requires the President to report to Congress any introduction of forces into hostilities or imminent hostilities, Section 4(a)(1); into foreign territory while equipped for combat, Section 4(a)(2); or in numbers which substantially enlarge U.S. forces equipped for combat already in a foreign nation, Section 4(a)(3). Once a report is submitted "or required to be submitted" under Section 4(a)(1), Congress must authorize the use of force within 60 to 90 days or the forces must be withdrawn. Since the War Powers Resolution's enactment in 1973, every President has taken the position that this statute is an unconstitutional infringement by the Congress on the President's authority as Commander in Chief. The courts have not directly addressed this question, even though lawsuits have been filed relating to the War Powers Resolution and its constitutionality.

Some recent operations—in particular U.S. participation in North Atlantic Treaty Organization (NATO) military operations in Kosovo, and in UN-authorized operations in Bosnia and Herzegovina, in the 1990s—have raised questions concerning whether NATO operations and/or UN-authorized operations are exempt from the requirements of the War Powers Resolution.

Regarding NATO operations, Article 11 of the North Atlantic Treaty states that its provisions are to be carried out by the parties "in accordance with their respective constitutional processes," implying that NATO Treaty commitments do not override U.S. constitutional provisions regarding the role of Congress in determining the extent of U.S. participation in NATO missions.

Section 8(a) of the War Powers Resolution states specifically that authority to introduce U.S. forces into hostilities is not to be inferred from any treaty, ratified before or after 1973, unless implementing legislation specifically authorizes such introduction and says it is intended to constitute an authorization within the meaning of the War Powers Resolution.

Regarding UN-authorized operations, for "Chapter VII" operations, undertaken in accordance with Articles 42 and 43 of the UN Charter, Section 6 of the U.N. Participation Act, P.L. 79-264, as amended, authorizes the President to negotiate special agreements with the UN Security Council, subject to the approval of Congress, providing for the numbers and types of armed forces and facilities to be made available to the Security Council. Once the agreements have been concluded, the law states, further congressional authorization is not necessary. To date, no such agreements have been concluded.

Given these provisions of U.S. law, and the history of disagreements between the President and the Congress over Presidential authority to introduce U.S. military personnel into hostilities in the absence of prior congressional authorization for such actions, it seems likely that a Presidential effort to establish a "no-fly zone" on his own authority would be controversial. Controversy would be all the more likely if the President were to undertake action "pre-emptively" or in the absence of a direct military threat to the United States.

Since the War Powers Resolution gives the President the authority to launch U.S. military actions prior to receiving an authorization from the Congress for 60-90 days, it is possible that the President could direct U.S.

armed forces to take or support military actions in accordance with U.N. Security Council Resolutions, or in support of NATO operations, and then seek statutory authority for such actions from the Congress.

Costs[74]

Potential total costs of Operation Odyssey Dawn remain highly unpredictable because of uncertainty about the duration of the conflict and its outcome; the nature and duration of continuing U.S. involvement; and the extent to which allies may take responsibility for sustaining the mission. The initial phases of the operation involved a quite intensive campaign to destroy Libyan air defense capabilities, coupled with attacks on other Libyan military sites, some strikes against Libyan leadership targets, and bombing of Libyan forces advancing toward opposition-held cities. More recently, U.S. aircraft appear to be providing a degree of close air support to ground operations by armed opposition groups. Now NATO has agreed to take on leadership of the operation, including supervision of no-fly zone enforcement and other elements of the operation, but the specific division of responsibility between the United States and allies has not been fully explained.

U.S. costs of continued enforcement of a no-fly zone might be quite limited, since Libyan air operations appear to have ceased. U.S. expenses for maintaining a no-fly zone would be further constrained if allies carry out most of the ongoing air operations. U.S. contributions might then be restricted to providing surveillance and air operations control capabilities with Airborne Warning and Control System (AWACS) aircraft, for example, supplemented by other intelligence and communications activities and maintenance of reserve forces for additional missions. Even some of those capabilities could come from allies—NATO has AWACS aircraft as well. Moreover, many of the capabilities the United States would contribute under those circumstances are normally on station in the Mediterranean or nearby, so the incremental costs—i.e., expenses over and above normal operating costs—might be limited to begin with.

Conversely, U.S. costs might climb to the extent the mission involves continuing attacks on ground targets. In that case, U.S. strike aircraft might be preferred over allied forces, particularly because of extensive U.S. experience in recent conflicts and the precision strike capabilities of U.S. forces. Additional U.S. surveillance, command, and control assets, such as Joint Surveillance and Target Attack Radar System (JSTARS) aircraft, might also be assigned to the mission. Such missions might also put U.S. forces at greater risk, with losses of aircraft possible.

Historical Costs as a Guide

As a very rough guide to the range of possible costs, Table 2 shows the costs to the U.S. Government of a variety of air operations the from FY1991 to FY2003. Of these, Operation Noble Anvil, the air war in Yugoslavia designed to contain a conflict in Kosovo, was the most intense. It involved initially limited and later extensive attacks to degrade air defenses throughout the Federal Republic of Yugoslavia, including all of Serbia. Those were followed by escalating air attacks initially focused on the military infrastructure and later on strategic targets. The operation lasted for two and a half months, from March 24 through June 10, 1999. The operation— including the no-fly zone and extensive additional activities—cost a total of $1.8 billion.

Toward the lower end of the spectrum are costs of the two no-fly zone operations in Iraq. The costs to the U.S. Government of Operation Southern Watch (OSW) averaged somewhat more than $700 million per year, or $60 million a month, although the amounts varied substantially from year to year. Costs of Operation Northern Watch (ONW) averaged about $123 million a year, or $10 million a month. The OSW mission required coverage of a relatively large geographic area, punctuated by occasional strikes against Iraqi air defense sites. U.S. aircraft were not necessarily always in the air, however, since they were based close to Iraqi airspace. The operation imposed a considerable burden on U.S. Air Force units, mainly because of its long duration.

Perhaps in the middle of the spectrum, at least in cost, are air operations in Bosnia-Herzegovina in the mid-1990s. Operation Joint Endeavor, carried out under the auspices of the Implementation Force (IFOR) from December 1995 to December 1996, involved a similar range of air operations as the current mission in Libya. Air operations included enforcement of a no-fly zone, attacks on Bosnian-Serb military forces, and close air support for Croatian ground operations. The combination of air and ground operations ultimately may have helped shift the balance of power in Bosnia enough to foster a political settlement. Air Force and Navy costs (though not entirely limited to air operations), totaled $298 million in FY1995 and $446 million in FY1996. IFOR operations continued for only the first three months of FY1996, so air operation costs appear quite substantial.

Whether the costs of these earlier operations provide a reasonable basis of comparison with current costs is uncertain. Inflation in itself would increase costs by about 50%. Current costs for comparable operations may also be higher today. Military personnel today are about 50% more expensive, after adjusting for inflation, than in the late 1990s, and operation and maintenance costs have also grown by about 50% above inflation over the past 15 years.

Costs of Initial Libyan Operations

While the Department of Defense (DOD) has released some details about operations conducted as of March 25, 2011, DOD has not identified the cost of initial operations to suppress Libyan air defenses, protect civilians, and establish a no-fly zone. Some press reports have cited a recent study by the Center for Strategic and Budgetary Assessments, which estimated the cost of initial operations and the cost of establishing and continuing a no-fly zone using various top-down methods and historical costs.[75] This study estimates that initial operations could run between $500 million and $1 billion, based on attacks on some 250 to 500 targets, and that the ongoing cost of a no-fly zone could range from $15 million to $300 million a week depending on the area of Libya that would be covered.[76]

Using operational details provided by DOD and DOD cost factors, a "bottoms-up" estimate of the cost of initial operations suggests that in the first six days of operations, DOD has spent roughly $400 million. The bulk of these costs reflect potential replacement costs for the Tomahawk missiles launched from Navy ships and the Joint Direct Attack Munitions (JDAMs) dropped by B-2 bombers at the beginning of the operation to suppress Libyan air defenses (about $260 million), and for the loss of a F-15E strike fighter aircraft over Libya because of mechanical failures ($75 million replacement cost). This estimate may not capture all costs of these initial operations.

Together, these hardware costs total about $335 million, or about 90% of the estimated total (see Table 1). The $260 million cost to replace the munitions expended in suppressing Libyan air defenses would be about 70% of the total estimated expenditures. Unless Libya is able to reconstitute its air defense network and airfields, these costs are unlikely to be repeated. Further, DOD spokesmen have suggested that the establishment of a no-fly zone is largely complete, and the United States is turning over that operation to the allies.[77]

DOD may or may not request additional funds to replace this hardware. It is not clear whether either the F-15 lost or all of the Tomahawk missiles expended would qualify as war-related expenses. Since 2009, DOD has been following new criteria for war-related funding, which prohibit requests for procurement items which are already scheduled for replacement.[78] The Air

Force expects to replace F-15E fighter aircraft with Joint Strike Fighters and some of the Tomahawk missiles used were of an older variant which is being replaced with a new version. The Navy may not need to replace all those expended, as some of the missiles used were of the older variant that is currently being replaced. The Navy is currently buying some 196 new Tomahawk missiles to expand the size of its current inventory.[79]

To replace the expended munitions, DOD could either re-direct funds from another source; request additional funds from Congress to replace the 168 Navy Tomahawk missiles and 45 Air Force JDAMs expended; or accept the reduced inventory levels resulting from their use.

Although DOD could request about $75 million to replace the lost F-15E, the Air Force budget includes funds each year for attrition in its aircraft inventory, which may already cover that cost.

The remaining $40 million, or about 10% of the total, are operational or military personnel costs for conducting combat air patrols and strike missions using F-15E, F-16, and AV-8B fighter aircraft, along with their support aircraft (e.g., tankers for refueling, electronic warfare support, and search and rescue aircraft.) Most of the operational costs are being paid for out of the Air Force's FY2011 Operations & Maintenance (O&M) account, which includes some $21.0 billion dedicated to training for combat operations and related support.[80] CRS does not assume any additional Navy ship operating costs because the Navy ordinarily keeps ships in the Mediterranean. The Navy reportedly agrees:

> According to [Chief of Naval Operations Admiral Gary] Roughead, the operations to date have not been particularly costly.
>
> "When you look at the expenses of what we in the Navy incurred, given the fact that we were already there, those costs are 'sunk' for me," he said. "I'm already paying for that."
>
> Thus far, expenses include additional flying hours and Tomahawk missiles used in the strikes, the admiral said.[81]

DOD may eventually decide that some of these costs are incremental—or additional to the Navy's normal presence missions.

Projecting future costs based on current operational costs could be problematic because costs to date reflect the high operating tempo of initial operations to neutralize Libyan air defenses, and are unlikely to be repeated now that the no-fly zone is in place. The United States has negotiated arrangements by which allies are assuming the bulk of coalition operations to maintain a no-fly zone with the U.S. confining its contribution to maintaining air surveillance with AWACS and other aircraft.

Table 1. Estimated Costs of Libyan Operations, March 19-March 24, 2011

	OPERATIONAL COSTS		
Initial Air Suppression	Flying Hoursa	Cost per flying hour	Estimated Cost in millions of $
Initial Suppression of Air Defenses			
B-2 bomber aircraft	75	31,236	2.3
Refueling support	84	9,031	0.8
Ongoing Combat Air Patrols and Strike Operations			
F-15Es	580	19,568	11.3
F-16s	580	8,926	5.2
Support Sorties			
EA-18G Growler electronic warfare	249	18,334	4.6
KC-135 refueling support	812	11,462	9.3
E-3 AWACS and E-8 JSTARS Intelligence,	84	18,648	1.6
Surveillance and Reconnaissance (ISR)			
EC-130J Commando Solo information operations/psychological operations	98	6,982	0.7
Search and Rescue Support	481	5,659	2.7
One-time Rescue Operation for F-15 lost			
Harriers, CH-53 helicopters, MV-22s, and KC-	10	Not applicable	0.1
130J			
SUBTOTAL OPERATIONS	2,894	Not applicable	38.6
POTENTIAL MILITARY PERSONNEL COSTS			
	No. Eligible	Monthly Amount	Total
Imminent Danger Payb	15,000	225	0.8
SUBTOTAL MILITARY PERSONNEL	15,000	225	0.8
POTENTIAL REPLACEMENT COSTSc			
Investment Costs	No. Expended	Cost per aircraft/missile	Estimated Cost
Replacing Tomahawk missiles	184	1,400	257.6
Replacing JDAM missiles	45	35,000	1.6
Replacement cost of lost F-15E	1	75,000,000	75.0
SUBTOTAL REPLACEMENT	Not applicable	Not applicable	334.2
TOTAL POTENTIAL COST			373.6

Sources: Department of Defense, Operational briefing including slides from March 19. 2011 through March 24, 2011; For total, and split between strike and support flying hours, and number of Tomahawks expended, CRS used slides in March 27, 2011 briefing; for flying hour cost by type of aircraft, used Air Force regulation, and proxies for Navy aircraft. For potential cost of replacing Tomahawks, used

FY2012 Department of the Navy, Budget Justification, Weapons Procurement, Navy.

[a] Flying hours estimated by number of sorties and length per sortie.

[b] The amount of Imminent Danger Pay depends on how the Department of Defense defines the Area of Responsibility (AOR) for Libyan operations. This estimate uses a rough estimate of the number of service members participating in the operation who are stationed on ships in the Mediterranean as well as those flying B-2 bombers from the United States; personnel contributing by providing command and control from home stations would not be included. Imminent danger pay is $250 additional per month but is pro-rated.

[c] Since 2009, the policy for defining war-related costs has been tightened, including a requirement that DOD cannot request replacement of combat losses for items that are already scheduled for replacement. This could eliminate the request for a replacement for the F-15 aircraft lost and reduce the number of see OMB, "Criteria for War/Overseas Contingency Operations Funding Request," February 26, 2009.

Other Issues for Congress

Other questions Congress may address include:

- What are the United States' strategic objectives in Libya?
- Who are the anti-Qadhafi forces? Is their success in the United States' national interest?
- Has Operation Odyssey Dawn directly or indirectly helped the anti-Qadhafi forces?
- How well did coalition coordination work, particularly given the short time available between the passage of UNSCR 1973 and the initiation of operations?
- What are the possible alternative political outcomes in Libya, and to what extent have military operations shaped those possibilities?

Table 2. Costs of Selected U.S. Combat Air Operations, FY1993-FY2003 (amounts in millions of current year dollars)

	FY1993	FY1994	FY1995	FY1996	FY1997	FY1998	FY1999	FY2000	FY2001	FY2002	FY2003
Southwest Asia											
Provide Comfort/Northern Watch	116.6	91..8	138.2	88..9	93.1	136.0	156.4	143.7	138.7		
										952.1	923.1
Southern Watch	715.9	333.0	468.4	576.3	597.3	1,497.2	933.2	755.4	678.0		
Desert Fox (Air Strikes, Dec. 1998)							92.9				
Former Yugoslavia (Bosnia)											
IFOR/SFOR/Joint-Deliberate Forge, Air Force & Navy		237.6	298.0	446.0	327.2						
Former Yugoslavia (Kosovo)											
Balkan Calm (Observer Mission, Pre- War)							34.6				
Eagle Eye (Air Verification, 10/98-3/99)							20.3				
Noble Anvil (Air War, 3/24-6/10/99							1,775.7				

Source: CRS based on data provided by Department of Defense, Office of the Under Secretary of Defense Comptroller.

End Notes

[1] This section was prepared by Christopher Blanchard, Acting Section Research Manager, and Jeremiah Gertler, Specialist in Military Aviation.

[2] United Nations Security Council, SC/10187/Rev. 1, "In Swift, Decisive Action, Security Council Imposes Tough Measures on Libyan Regime, Adopting Resolution 1970 in Wake of Crackdown on Protesters," February 26, 2011, http://www.un.org/News/Press/docs/2011/sc10187.doc.htm, accessed March 18, 2011.

[3] Thomas E. Ricks, "Gates lays out criteria for Libya action," *ForeignPolicy.com/Best Defense blog*, March 10, 2011.

[4] Remarks by Ambassador Susan E. Rice, U.S. Permanent Representative to the United Nations, at the Security Council Stakeout on Libya, New York, NY, March 16, 2011.

[5] Frank Oliveri, "Top Officer Says 'No-Fly' Zone Over Libya Might Not Help Rebels," *CQ Today Online*, March 17, 2011.

[6] U.S. Congress, Senate Committee on Armed Services, *Hearing on the Proposed Fiscal 2012 and Future Year Defense Authorization Budget Request Related to the Air Force*, 112th Cong., 1st sess., March 17, 2011.

[7] President Barack Obama, Remarks by the President on the Situation in Libya, March 18, 2011. Available at http://www.whitehouse.gov/the-press-office/2011/03/18/remarks-president

[8] President Barack Obama, Letter from the President Regarding the Commencement of Operations in Libya, March 21, 2011. Available at http://www.whitehouse.gov/the-press-office/2011/03/21/letter-president-

[9] Reuters, "UN Security Council authorizes no-fly zone over Libya," March 18, 2011.

[10] OSC Report GMP20110314950010, "Arab League Urges U.N. to Impose No-Fly Zone Over Libya," March 12, 2011.

[11] There are conflicting reports from unnamed Arab official sources that some governments opposed the decision. On March 17, Algerian diplomats informed CRS that their government did not oppose the Arab League Council decision, contrary to some press reports. Algeria has urged coordination with the African Union, stressed that any no-fly zone decision must be taken by the U.N. Security Council, and maintains its general "opposition to any foreign intervention in Libya," a position it maintained with regard to uprising in Tunisia and Egypt. Syria's representative also is rumored to have expressed reservations about the decision and has warned against foreign intervention in Libya.

[12] Raghida Dergham, "Interview with Amr Moussa: The Goal in Libya Is Not Regime Change," *International Herald Tribune*, March 23, 2011.

[13] Testimony of Undersecretary of State William Burns, before the Senate Foreign Relations Committee, March 17, 2011.

[14] European Commission, "The European Commission's humanitarian response to the crisis in Libya," Memo/11/143, March 4, 2011.

[15] Simon Tisdall, "Germany blocks plans for Libya no-fly zone," *Guardian* (UK) March 15, 2011. On March 17, German Foreign Minister Guido Westerwelle said, "we won't take part in any military operation and I will not send German troops to Libya."

[16] On February 28, Turkish Prime Minister Recep Tayyip Erdoğan stated "NATO's intervention in Libya is out of the question," and on March 14, he stated that foreign military intervention in Libya's conflict, including NATO operations, "would be totally counter-productive" and "could have dangerous consequences." As of March 24, Turkey reportedly planned to contribute four frigates, a support vessel, and a submarine to NATO's Operation Unified Protector.

[17] This section was prepared by Jeremiah Gertler, Specialist in Military Aviation.
[18] DOD press briefing by Vice Admiral Bill Gortney, Director of the Joint Staff, March 19, 2011.
[19] "The Weapons We're Hitting Gadhafi With," *DefenseTech.org*, March 20, 2011.
[20] DOD press briefing by Rear Admirlal Gerald Hueber, March 23, 2011.
[21] Gen. James N. Mattis, commander, U.S. Central Command, in John Vandiver and Geoff Ziezulewicz, "No-fly zone over Libya: The facts," *Stars & Stripes*, March 1, 2011.
[22] Sean O'Connor, "The Libyan SAM Network," *IMINT & Analysis blog*, May 11, 2010.
[23] For comparison, the Libyan system is older and less sophisticated than the Iraqi air defense network that was neutralized by U.S. and allied forces early in Operation Desert Storm.
[24] Adm. Samuel Locklear, press briefing, March 22, 2011.
[25] Gen. Norton Schwartz, in testimony before the U.S. Congress, Senate Committee on Armed Services, *Testimony on the Department of the Air Force in review of the Defense Authorization*, 112th Cong., March 17, 2011.
[26] International Institute for Strategic Studies, "Chapter Seven: Middle East and North Africa," in *The Military Balance 2011*, 111th ed. (London: Brassey's, 2011).
[27] Ibid.
[28] "Malta refusing to return Libyan fighter jets, says it denied landing to plane carrying pilots," *Canadian Press*, March 1, 2011.
[29] DOD press briefing by Rear Admirlal Gerald Hueber, March 23, 2011.
[30] Martha Raddatz, Alexander Marquardt and Luis Martinez, "Gadhafi's Warplane Shot Down by French Fighter Jets in Misrata," *ABCNews.com*, March 24, 2011.
[31] General James F. Amos, in testimony before the U.S. Congress, House Committee on Armed Services, *Testimony on the Department of the Navy in review of the Defense Authorization,* 112th Cong., March 1, 2011.
[32] Andy Nativi, "Italy: Doing More than Playing Host for Libyan Operations," *AviationWeek/Ares blog*, March 21, 2011.
[33] DOD press briefing by Rear Admirlal Gerald Hueber, March 23, 2011.
[34] Ibid.
[35] John A. Tirpak, "Odyssey Dawn Units Identified," *Air Force Association Daily Report*, March 22, 2011, "Fairchild tankers handle Libya refueling duties," *Associated Press*, March 22, 2011, and DOD press briefing by Vice Admiral Bill Gortney, Director of the Joint Staff, March 28, 2011.
[36] John A. Tirpak, "Odyssey Dawn Units Identified," *Air Force Association Daily Report*, March 22, 2011.
[37] DOD press briefing by Vice Admiral Bill Gortney, Director of the Joint Staff, March 19, 2011 and "The Weapons We're Hitting Gadhafi With," *DefenseTech.org*, March 20, 2011.
[38] 26th Marine Expeditionary Unit, "26th MEU rescues U.S. Air Force pilots after plane crash," undated press release.
[39] Ibid.
[40] Christian Lowe, "Growlers Over Libya—An Update," *DefenseTech.org*, March 23, 2011 and Marina Malenic, "Navy EW Plane Makes Combat Debut Over Libya," *Defense Daily*, March 24, 2011.
[41] "Global Hawk Drone and E-8 JSTARS May Be Helping the Libya Fight," *DefenseTech.org*, March 22, 2011.
[42] Robert Wall, "No-Fly Zone Fighter Force Expands," *AviationWeek/Ares blog*, March 2011; Paul McLeary, "Canada Patrolling Over Libyan Coast," *AviationWeek/Ares blog*, March 21, 2011; "The Weapons We're Hitting Gadhafi With," *DefenseTech.org*, March 20, 2011; Robert Wall, "Libya: Charles de Gaulle Embarked Rafales Engage; Dutch Sign Up, Sort

Of," *AviationWeek/Ares blog*, March 23, 2011; Pierre Tran, "UAE Fighter Jets Join Coalition Campaign in Libya," *Defense News.com*, March 25, 2011.

[43] DOD press briefing by Vice Admiral Bill Gortney, Director of the Joint Staff, March 19, 2011; "The Weapons We're Hitting Gadhafi With," *DefenseTech.org*, March 20, 2011; Robert Wall, "Libya: Charles de Gaulle Embarked Rafales Engage; Dutch Sign Up, Sort Of," *AviationWeek/Ares blog*, March 23, 2011.

[44] DOD press briefing by Vice Admiral Bill Gortney, Director of the Joint Staff, March 19, 2011.

[45] This section was prepared by Lauren Ploch, Analyst in African Affairs.

[46] DOD press briefing by Admiral Samuel J. Locklear III, commander, Joint Task Force Odyssey Dawn, March 22, 2011.

[47] DOD press briefing by Vice Admiral Bill Gortney, Director of the Joint Staff, March 24, 2011.

[48] DOD press briefing by Rear Admiral Gerald Hueber, March 23, 2011.

[49] DOD press briefing by Vice Admiral Bill Gortney, Director of the Joint Staff, March 24, 2011.

[50] NATO, "Statement by NATO Secretary General Anders Fogh Rasmussen on Libya," press release, March 27, 2011, http://www.nato.int/cps/en/SID-D728658D-B13DAF92/natolive/news_71808.htm.

[51] Slobodan Lekic, "NATO to assume command of Libya air operations," *Associated Press*, March 27, 2011.

[52] This section was prepared by Paul Belkin, Analyst in European Affairs, and Derek E. Mix, Analyst in European Affairs.

[53] As of March 24, 2011, Belgium, Canada, Denmark, France, Italy, Norway, Spain, and the United Kingdom had deployed fighter planes to the region. Turkey had committed naval assets to the NATO mission to enforce the UN arms embargo.

[54] See NATO, "NATO Secretary General's statement on Libya no-fly zone," http://www.nato.int/cps/en/SID-33554D48-EEFB8A0C/natolive/news_71763.htm; and U.S. Department of State, *Update on Implementing UN Security Council Resolutions 1970 and 1973 on Libya*—Remarks by Hillary Rodham Clinton, March 24, 2011 http://www.state

[55] "Sarkozy: Gaddafi must step down," PressTV, February 25, 2011; Ian Black, "World sends message to Gaddafi: it is time to end your regime," *The Guardian*, February 28, 2011; interviews of French officials, March 2011.

[56] See "Sarkozy's Libyan Surprise," *The Economist*, March 14, 2011.

[57] In addition to Secretary of State Hillary Rodham Clinton, the meeting was attended by the prime ministers or foreign ministers of Belgium, Canada, Denmark, France, Germany, Italy, Morocco, Norway, Poland, Qatar, Spain, the United Arab Emirates, and the UK, as well as representatives of the Arab League, the EU, and the UN.

[58] See, for example, David Kirkpatrick et. al., "Allies Open Air Assault on Qaddafi's Forces in Libya," *New York Times*, March 19, 2011.

[59] See, for example, Ian Traynor and Nicholas Watt, "Libya no-fly zone leadership squabbles continue within NATO," *The Guardian*, March 23, 2011; and "Still No Decision Who Will Oversee Libya Strikes," *Agence France-Presse*, March 22, 2011.

[60] In what was portrayed as an effort to ease the allied burden in other NATO operations, German Chancellor Angela Merkel's cabinet agreed on March 23 to take over command of AWACS surveillance operations in Afghanistan with a deployment of an additional 300 military personnel to the country.

[61] A harmattan is a "hot, dry wind that blows from the northeast or east in the western Sahara." "Harmattan," in *Encyclopedia Britannica Online*.

[62] French Ministry of Defense, *"Libye: point de situation de l'operation Harmattan #3,"* http://www.defense.gouv.fr/operations/autres-operations/operation-harmattan-libye/actualites.

[63] Karen DeYoung and Edward Cody, "On Libya, France's president steps forward to assume spotlight," *Washington Post*, March 25, 2011.

[64] "Ellamy" is a name "randomly generated by a computer programme." "Libya: What do the military operation names mean?," *BBC online*, March 24, 2011.

[65] See the UK Ministry of Defence's online suite of resources about Operation Ellamy, http://www.mod.uk/DefenceInternet/DefenceNews/InDepth/LibyaOperationEllamy.htm. See also http://www.defense-aerospace.com/ articles-view/release/3/123815/raf-typhoons-join-libyan-no_fly-zone-patrols.html.

[66] Thomas Harding, "Libya: Navy running short of Tomahawk missiles," *The Daily Telegraph*, March 23, 2011. The article estimates the cost of operating four Tornados and three Eurofighters plus support aircraft at over £3.2 million per day (approximately $5.1 million), plus £1.1 million per Storm Shadow missile (approximately $1.75 million) and £800,000 (approximately $1.3 million) per Tomahawk missile.

[67] The Italian airbases reportedly opened to coalition use are Amendola, Gioia del Colle, Sigonella, Aviano, Trapani, and Decimomannu. Italy also hosts an important NATO headquarters, Joint Force Command Naples.

[68] "Libyan Operation 'Must Not Be War, Says Italy," ANSA, March 21, 2011; "Italy 'Suppresses Enemy Defences' in Libya: Military," AFP, March 21, 2011; "Europe Divided Over Allied Campaign in Libya" AFP, March 21, 2011.

[69] "Canadian patrol planes to join Libya mission," *CBC News*, March 24, 2011.

[70] Carina O'Reilly, "Belgium to Send Troops to Join Libyan Intervention," IHS Global Insight Daily Analysis, March 21, 2011; Belgian Ministry of Defense, *"Vier F-16s in Libi ,"* March 22, 2011, http://www.mil.be; articles from *The Copenhagen Post* accessed on http://www.denmark.dk, "Libya blames Denmark for attack, No bombs from Danish jets in Libya, and F-16s readied to defend Libyan people," March 22, 2011.

[71] "Norway wants command decision before starting Libya ops," *AFP*, March 21, 2011.

[72] NATO Fact Sheet, *NATO Arms Embargo against Libya Operation Unified Protector*, March 25, 2011 http://www.nato.int/nato_static/assets NATO Press Briefing with Brigadier General Pierre St-Amand, Canadian Air Force and General Massimo Panizzi, spokesperson of the Chairman of the Military Committee, March 23, 2011, http://www.nato.int/cps/en/SID-83A5384E-C37D94AC/natolive/opinions_71716.htm?selectedLocale=en.

[73] This section was prepared by Richard Grimmett, Specialist in International Security.

[74] This section was prepared by Stephen Daggett, Specialist in Defense Policy and Budgets, and Amy Belasco, Specialist in U.S. Defense Policy and Budget.

[75] National Journal, Daily PM Update, March 21, 2011 by Megan Scully; http://www.nationaljournal.com/nationalsecurity/costs-of-libya-operation-already-piling-up-20110321?page=2.

[76] Center for Strategic and Budgetary Assessments, "Selected Options and Costs for a No-Fly Zone over Libya," by Todd Harrison & Zack Cooper, March 2011, p. 4 and p.7; http://www.csbaonline.org/wp-content/uploads/2011/03/2011.03.09-Libya-No-Fly-Zone.pdf.

[77] News Transcript; "Presenter: NBC's David Gregory, Secretary of Defense Robert M. Gates, and Secretary of State Hillary Clinton," March 27, 2011; http://www.defense.gov/landing/comment.aspx.

[78] OMB, "Criteria for War/Overseas Contingency Operations Funding Request," February 26, 2009. The relevant language is "Replacement only of items not already scheduled for replacement in the Future Years Defense Plan – no accelerations; " and "Replacement of munitions expended in theater if existing stocks are inadequate."

[79] Department of the Navy, FY2012 Budget Estimates, Weapons Procurement, Navy; see Exhibit P-40 Exhibit, p. 20; http://www.finance.hq.navy.mil/FMB/12pres/WPN_BOOK.PDF.

[80] Department of the Air Force, *Fiscal Year (FY) 2012 Budget Justification, Operation and Maintenance*, Exhibit O-1P, p. 10, see Budget Activity 1; http://www.saffm.hq.af.mil/shared/media

[81] Marina Malenic, "Navy EW Plane Makes Combat Debut Over Libya," *Defense Daily*, March 24, 2011.

In: Libya
Editors: B. L. Kerr and M. I. Cantu
ISBN: 978-1-61942-615-3

Chapter 2

LIBYA: TRANSITION AND U.S. POLICY*

Christopher M. Blanchard

SUMMARY

After more than 40 years of authoritarian repression and eight months of armed conflict, fundamental political change has come to Libya. The killing of Muammar al Qadhafi on October 20 and the declaration of Libya's liberation by the interim Transitional National Council on October 23 marked the end of the Libyan people's armed struggle and the formal beginning of the country's transition to a new political order. Overcoming the legacy of Qadhafi's rule and the effects of the recent fighting is now the principal challenge for the Libyan people, the TNC, and the international community. The transition period may prove to be as complex and challenging for Libyans and their international counterparts as the recent conflict. Immediate tasks include establishing and maintaining security, preventing criminality and reprisals, restarting Libya's economy, and taking the first steps in a planned transition to democratic governance. In the coming weeks and months, Libyans will face key questions about basic terms for transitional justice, a new constitutional order, political participation, and Libyan foreign policy. Security challenges, significant investment needs, and vigorous political debates are now emerging.

---

* This is an edited, reformatted and augmented version of a Congressional Research Service publication, CRS Report for Congress RL33142, from www.crs.gov, dated October 25, 2011.

The U.S. military continues to participate in Operation Unified Protector, the North Atlantic Treaty Organization (NATO) military operation to enforce United Nations (U.N.) Security Council Resolution 1973, which authorizes "all necessary measures" to protect Libyan civilians. On October 23, NATO leaders indicated that the military operation would draw to a close on October 31, barring any unforeseen developments that require its continuation. U.S. officials express confidence that nuclear materials and chemical weapons components that are stored in Libya remain secure and state that remote monitoring will continue. The proliferation of military weaponry from unsecured Libyan stockpiles—including small arms, explosives, and shoulder-fired anti-aircraft missiles—remains a serious concern. The Obama Administration is implementing a program with the TNC to retrieve and disable certain weapons and has reiterated that it has no intention of deploying U.S. military forces on the ground in Libya. The U.S. Embassy in Tripoli has reopened with a limited staff. Congress may consider proposals for further assisting Libya's transitional authorities or supporting security efforts.

The U.N. General Assembly has recognized the TNC as Libya's U.N. representative, and the Security Council adopted Resolution 2009, creating a three-month mandate for a U.N. Support Mission in Libya (UNSMIL) to assist Libyans with public security and transition arrangements. The resolution also sets conditions for the sale of arms and training to the Libyan government and partially lifts the U.N. mandated asset freeze for certain purposes. The TNC continues to call for the release of Libyan assets seized pursuant to Resolutions 1970 and 1973. Transfers of assets have begun from multiple governments, including $1.5 billion in previously blocked assets that the U.S. government has arranged to support Libyan humanitarian, fuel, and salary needs. U.S. Treasury Department licenses now authorize the release of assets belonging to some Libyan entities and allow some transactions with some Libyan state institutions, including oil companies.

A TNC stabilization team is leading Libyan efforts to deliver services; assess reconstruction needs; and begin to reform ministries, public utilities, and security forces. The TNC has issued orders concerning security and established a high security council to coordinate volunteer forces. Initial reports from Libya suggest that local militias and some emergent political groups may oppose certain TNC policies and seek to replace certain TNC personalities. TNC officials remain confident in Libyan unity, and an interim government is expected to replace the TNC executive authority within a month. As Libyans work to shape their future, Congress and the Administration will have the first opportunity to fully redefine U.S.-Libyan relations since the 1960s.

BACKGROUND

Political change in neighboring Tunisia and Egypt helped bring long-simmering Libyan reform debates to the boiling point in January and early February 2011. In recent years, leading Libyans had staked out a broad range of positions about the necessary scope and pace of reform, while competing for influence and opportunity under the watchful eye of hard-liners aligned with the enigmatic leader of Libya's September 1969 revolution, Muammar al Qadhafi. Qadhafi had long insisted that he held no formal government position, but by all accounts he maintained his 40- plus-year hold on ultimate authority, until recently, as the "reference point" for Libya's byzantine political system. Ironically, that system cited "popular authority" as its foundational principle and organizing concept, but it denied Libyans the most basic political rights. Tribal relations and regional dynamics, particularly long-held resentments of Qadhafi among residents in the east, also influence Libyan politics. Rivalries are emerging among locally organized revolutionary groups with differing experiences during Qadhafi's rule and the recent conflict. Political groups with differing priorities will also shape Libya's transition (see "Political Dynamics" below).

Qadhafi government policy reversals on weapons of mass destruction (WMD) and terrorism led to the lifting of most international sanctions in 2003 and 2004, followed by economic liberalization, oil sales, and foreign investment that brought new wealth to some in Libya. U.S. business gradually reengaged amid continuing U.S.-Libyan tension over terrorism concerns that were finally resolved in 2008. During this period of international reengagement, political change in Libya remained elusive and illusory. Some observers argued that Qadhafi supporters' suppression of opposition had softened, as Libya's international rehabilitation coincided with steps by some pragmatists to maneuver within so-called "red lines." The shifting course of those red lines had been increasingly entangling reformers in the run-up to the outbreak of unrest in February 2011. Government rehabilitation of imprisoned Islamist militants and the return of some exiled opposition figures were welcomed by some observers. Ultimately, inaction on the part of the government in response to calls for guarantees of basic political rights and for the drafting of a constitution suggested a lack of consensus, if not outright opposition to meaningful reform.

The recent conflict was triggered in mid-February 2011 by a chain of events in Benghazi and other eastern cities that quickly spiraled out of Qadhafi's control. The government's loss of control over key eastern cities became apparent in mid-February, and broader unrest emerged in other regions. A number of military officers, their units, and civilian officials abandoned Qadhafi for the cause of the then-disorganized and amorphous opposition. Qadhafi and his supporters denounced their opponents as drug-fueled traitors, foreign agents, and Al Qaeda supporters. Until August, Qadhafi and allied forces maintained control over the capital, Tripoli, and other cities. The cumulative effects of attrition by NATO airstrikes against military targets and a coordinated offensive by rebels in Tripoli and from across western Libya then turned the tide, sending Qadhafi and his supporters into retreat and exile. September and early October were marked by sporadic and often intense fighting with Qadhafi supporters in and around Qadhafi's birthplace, Sirte, and the town of Bani Walid and neighboring military districts. NATO air operations continued as rebel fighters engaged in battles of attrition with Qadhafi supporters.

Qadhafi's death at the hands of rebel fighters in Sirte on October 23 brought the conflict to an abrupt close, with some observers expressing concern that a dark chapter in Libyan history ended violently, with an uncertain path ahead.

STATUS AS OF OCTOBER 25, 2011

On October 23, interim Transitional National Council (TNC) chief Mustafa Abdeljalil announced the liberation of Libya and stated that an interim government would be named within one month. Accordingly, NATO-led military operations to enforce U.N. Security Council Resolution 1970 and 1973 are drawing to a close, and may end by October 31.[1] NATO air and sea patrol operations continue, with no air-to-ground strikes reported since October 20. The rebel capture of the Qadhafi military compound at Bab al Aziziyah in the capital Tripoli on August 23 signaled the symbolic end of Qadhafi's reign. Qadhafi's death outside of his hometown of Sirte on the central coast on October 20 brought an end to the fighting that had continued in isolated areas of central and southern Libya between Qadhafi supporters and rebel forces. It is not immediately apparent whether any remaining Qadhafi supporters will seek to rekindle an irregular warfare campaign against the TNC, although the possibility of fighting among rebel factions exists.

The TNC has asserted nominal control over developments in Tripoli and has begun the task of coordinating the diverse collection of armed groups that made the rebel capture of the city possible, but which did not previously necessarily coordinate their actions with the TNC or each other. A "high security council" serves as a coordinating mechanism for disparate volunteer groups and regime defectors, including armed factions from communities like Zintan and Misuratah and those led by Islamist figures, such as former Libyan Islamic Fighting Group commander Abdelhakim Belhajj (see "Libyan Islamic Fighting Group (LIFG)/Libyan Islamic Movement for Change (LIMC)" below).[2]

TNC figures have issued repeated calls for armed groups and citizens to avoid destruction of public property, looting, and reprisals, in a conscious effort to avoid some of the immediate security problems that plagued Iraq in the wake of the collapse of Saddam Hussein's government. The TNC has signaled its intention to take a inclusive approach with regard to government personnel not known to have been involved in severe human rights violations or public corruption. The success of the TNC initiatives and the acceptability of this approach among Libyans remains to be seen. TNC officials remain concerned about their ability to provide services and maintain security, although the resumption of water service in Tripoli, deliveries of fuel, and infusions of seized assets have improved their position. TNC leaders estimate that over 20,000 Libyans have been killed in the recent conflict, with a further 50,000 injured.[3] These statistics have not been independently verified by any international third party.

Qadhafi's Death, Liberation, and Interim Government

The death of Muammar al Qadhafi, his son Mutassim al Qadhafi, and defense official Abu Bakr Yunis Jabr near Sirte on October 20 brought a dramatic end to the conflict and signaled the irreversibility of political change to Libyans and the international community. Nevertheless, the uncertain circumstances of Qadhafi's death have raised questions about the accountability of armed groups in Libya and the TNC's nascent control over the country—video footage appeared to show Qadhafi wounded, but alive in rebel custody prior to his subsequent death by a gunshot wound. TNC officials have promised to investigate the events leading up to Qadhafi's death, amid calls from human rights organizations and other international actors for a full public inquiry.

The formal announcement of Libya's liberation by TNC leader Mustafa Abdeljalil opened a new chapter in Libyan political life and illustrated many of the questions and themes that appear likely to shape the transition period. For example, mild controversy over the TNC's choice of location for the announcement—Benghazi—reflects simmering rivalries among locally organized revolutionary groups for influence over national affairs. Some Libyans argued that Tripoli may have been a more appropriate location for the declaration, while other observers questioned whether security concerns in the capital show that the TNC's authority is more limited than many outsiders assume.

The content of Abdeljalil's statement also has attracted domestic and international interest, particularly his emphasis on the population's Islamic character and the extent to which Libyan law may be based on religious law in the future. In his remarks, Abdeljalil stated that "We, as a Muslim state, have taken the Islamic sharia as the main source of legislation, and therefore, any law which contravenes the Islamic principles of sharia, is legally void." He gave as examples policies prohibiting men from marrying more than one wife and allowing interest-based financial transactions. The draft charter that the TNC has proposed to guide the interim transition period states that "Islam is the religion of the state and the principal source of legislation is Islamic jurisprudence (*sharia*).... The State shall guarantee for non-Moslems the freedom of practicing religious rights and shall guarantee respect for their systems of personal status." (See "Interim Transitional National Council (TNC)" and "Transitional National Council Positions and Statements" below.)

Congressional Action and Legislation

Many Members of Congress have welcomed the announcement of Libya's liberation and Qadhafi's death, while expressing concern about security in the country, the potential proliferation of Libyan weapons, and the prospects for a smooth political transition. The Senate version of the FY2012 State Department and Foreign Operations appropriations bill (S. 1601) would provide $20 million in bilateral Economic Support Fund (ESF) account assistance "to promote democracy, transparent and accountable governance, human rights, transitional justice, and the rule of law in Libya, and for exchange programs between Libyan and American students." The bill prohibits non-loan-based funding for rehabilitation or reconstruction of infrastructure in Libya. The committee report on the bill directs the use of Nonproliferation, Antiterrorism, Demining, and Related Programs (NADR) account funding for disarmament and securing Libyan weapons stockpiles. The Obama Administration has announced its intention to use $40 million in appropriated funds to support similar efforts that are now ongoing, with U.S. civilian advisers working with the TNC to locate, secure, and disable shoulder-fired missiles and other weaponry.

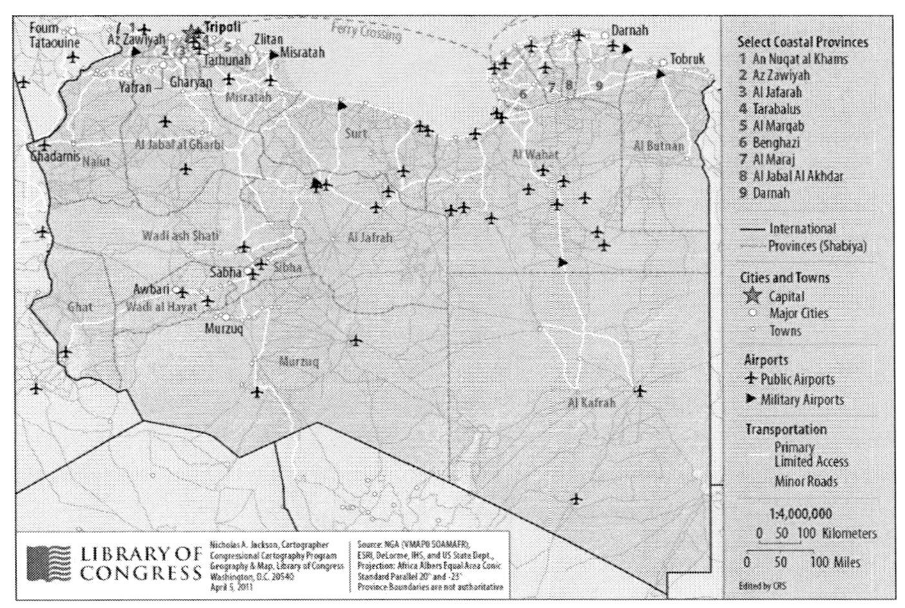

Sources: Congressional Cartography Program, Library of Congress, edited by CRS.

Figure 1. Political Map of Libya.

Some Members of Congress have suggested that some frozen Libyan assets should be directed, in consultation with Libyan authorities, toward reimbursement of NATO countries for military operations. Others are seeking to link the availability of assets frozen by the United States to Libyan cooperation with investigations into Qadhafi-era terrorist attacks. (See "Libyan Assets, TNC Funding, and Oil Exports" below.)

H.Con.Res. 75 would state the sense of Congress that

> the funds of the regime of Muammar Qaddafi that have been frozen by the United States should be returned to the people of Libya for their benefit, including humanitarian and reconstruction assistance, and the President should explore the possibility with the Transitional National Council of using some of such funds to reimburse NATO countries for expenses incurred in Operation Odyssey Dawn and Operation Unified Protector.

S. 1520 would restrict the transfer of blocked Libyan assets to Libyan authorities for other than humanitarian purposes until the President certifies to Congress "that the Transitional National Council or successor government is fully cooperating with requests for information and ongoing investigations related to the bombing of Pan Am flight 103 and any other terrorist attacks attributable to the government of Muammar Qaddafi against United States citizens." The bill would provide national security waiver authority to the President and require reporting on U.S. efforts to obtain information regarding terrorist attacks along with Libyan cooperation.

Debate between Congress and the Obama Administration about congressional authorization and the cost of U.S. military operations in Libya diminished as the prospect of a sustained military campaign requiring extended U.S. investment and force deployments became less likely. Some Members of Congress sought a clearer definition of U.S. objectives, costs, and operations, and, in June and July, some Members of Congress became increasingly assertive in their efforts to force President Barack Obama to seek congressional authorization for continued U.S. military involvement. A number of proposed resolutions and amendments to appropriations and authorization bills sought to require reporting on U.S. strategy and operations or to proscribe limits on the authorization or funding for continued U.S. military operations in Libya. Others sought to authorize the continued use of U.S. Armed Forces in support of NATO operations, short of the use of ground troops.

On June 3, the House adopted H.Res. 292 (Roll no. 411), which directed the Administration to provide documents on consultation with Congress and a report "describing in detail United States security interests and objectives, and the activities of United States Armed Forces, in Libya since March 19, 2011." The Administration submitted the report on June 15, 2011.[4] The House of Representatives rejected a series of other resolutions seeking to authorize or deauthorize continuing U.S. participation in Operation Unified Protector.

Assessment and Key Issues

The Obama Administration's stated policy objectives in Libya have been to protect civilians and to secure a democratic political transition, including the departure of Muammar al Qadhafi from power and the selection of a new government by the Libyan people. In pursuit of U.S. objectives, the Administration supported military, financial, and diplomatic efforts to enforce

United Nations Security Council Resolutions 1970 and 1973, both of which stopped short of calling for Qadhafi's removal. The Administration argued that sustained U.S. and international military and financial pressure would resolve core differences between U.S. and U.N.-endorsed goals by convincing remaining loyalists to withdraw their support for Qadhafi and opening the way for his departure and a settlement of the conflict. Qadhafi's intransigence notwithstanding, the combination of the opposition's military operations and international military and financial pressure appears to have succeeded in convincing many prominent regime figures to defect and ultimately in toppling the Qadhafi regime. The implications of this regime change for Libya, the region, and the United States remain to be seen.

The post-conflict Libyan political order will be complicated by the immediate consequences of the current fighting, the legacies of decades of Qadhafi's patronage- and fear-based rule, and the chronic economic and political challenges that have fueled popular discontent in recent years. Security is the immediate priority, and questions remain about the ability of the TNC to assert control. Prior to the capture of Tripoli, reports from eastern Libya suggested that limited financial resources and latent political rivalries were creating parallel challenges for the TNC as it sought to solidify its base of support among the disparate groups that rose up against Qadhafi. Those challenges are now reflected on a national scale.

The July 2011 assassination of rebel military commander and prominent regime defector Abdelfattah Younis al Ubaydi, reportedly by rival rebel forces, cast serious doubt on the unity of TNC-affiliated military forces and led to the resignation of several TNC leadership figures. Similarly, the controversy surrounding the killing of Qadhafi is reopening questions about military command and control among the revolutionaries. Various rebel groups have stated their recognition of the TNC's authority as a means of securing the country in the immediate aftermath of Qadhafi's fall. However, press reports and interviews suggest that these groups remain wary of each other in some cases, and some calls for changes to the leadership of the TNC have emerged from former rebel groups. TNC officials announced some leadership changes in early October, and an interim government is set to be formed within one month of the October 23 liberation announcement. U.S. officials have not yet indicated they regard the debates and delays as threats to Libya's transition.[5]

Paying salaries, purchasing imports, maintaining public utility services, and meeting administrative and military needs reportedly have tested the limited financial resources and expertise available to the TNC, although some reports suggest that recent infusions of previously frozen assets have reduced some of the financial pressure.[6] Both financial and administrative challenges have increased now that the TNC is seeking to pay salaries and assert control over Libya's major population center in Tripoli and manage government entities in the rest of the country. Some TNC leaders continue to cite financial constraints in public statements and urge foreign governments to fully release frozen Libyan assets. Some reports from visiting nongovernmental experts and State Department officials suggest that while a lively political atmosphere has emerged in opposition-controlled areas, political support for the TNC among the broader population may be contingent on the council's ability to provide basic services and financial support via salaries and subsidies.[7] Other key TNC and public concerns include providing medical care for wounded volunteer fighters and civilians and channeling financial support and relief supplies to individuals displaced or otherwise negatively effected by the conflict. Organized armed groups or ad hoc citizen coalitions may choose to challenge the TNC if public hardships increase or if TNC political decisions prove controversial. Taken together, these factors suggest that securing U.S. interests in Libya will require sustained attention and resources beyond the scope of the current fighting and emergent transition period.

United Nations Support Mission in Libya (UNSMIL) and Other Stabilization Efforts

The Administration has not publicly disclosed plans for U.S. participation in multilateral post-conflict security, stability, or reconstruction operations in Libya or highlighted requests for new funding to support such efforts by third-parties, including the new United Nations Support Mission in Libya (UNSMIL) established by Resolution 2009.[8] U.N. Secretary General Ban Ki-moon has named UK-born Ian Martin as the director for UNSMIL. Martin is continuing the work he began in mid-2011 as the Secretary General's special adviser for post-conflict and transition issues in Libya. A sector-by-sector post-conflict needs assessment is planned under the auspices of the TNC, the United Nations, the European Union, the World Bank, and the International Monetary Fund (IMF). A preliminary visit by World Bank and IMF officials took place in early October.

Conventional Weapons and Chemical and Nuclear Materials

The apparent proliferation of small arms, man-portable air defense missile systems (MANPADS), and some heavy weaponry among fighters on both sides of the recent conflict has led some counterterrorism and arms trafficking experts, as well as officials in neighboring countries, to express concern about the conflict's longer-term implications for regional security.[9] Most security experts expect that unexploded ordnance, explosive remnants, and looted weaponry will present a challenge inside Libya for an extended period of time. On May 9, the Administration notified Congress that it had waived normal congressional notification requirements to immediately obligate $1.5 million in Nonproliferation, Antiterrorism, Demining and Related Programs (NADR) account funding for "urgently needed assistance to collect, destroy, and reestablish control of Libyan munitions and small arms and light weapons" in response to "a substantial risk to human health or welfare."[10] The funding was provided to nongovernmental organizations specializing in international demining and ordnance disposal. Those organizations and others are working with the United Nations as part of a Joint Mine Action Coordination Team that issues regular reports on the status of efforts to remove ordnance threats across Libya and related funding needs.[11] As of October 2011, these efforts were being expanded through the efforts of a team of U.S. State Department advisers working in Libya with the TNC to secure weapons sites and to relocate and disable MANPADs. The Administration has announced plans to spend approximately $40 million on this effort, in consultation with Congress.

Regional Smuggling

Israeli officials have stated that "weapons are available in Libya as a result of the unstable situation there, and Hamas has exploited it to buy weapons from Libyan smugglers."[12] According to unnamed Israeli officials, "thousands" of weapons have entered Gaza from Libya, including "SA-7 anti-aircraft missiles and rocket-propelled grenades (RPGs)," but the weaponry is "not a major qualitative enhancement" for Gaza-based armed groups.[13] CRS cannot independently verify these statements, and the Obama Administration has not commented on the record regarding reports of arms shipments from Libya to Gaza. Authorities in other countries, including Egypt, Niger, Algeria, and Tunisia have expressed similar concerns. There is no indication that members of the TNC have been involved with reported shipments of weapons and material from Libya to Gaza or other countries since the uprising began.

Chemical Weapons and Nuclear Materials

The security of Libya's stockpiles of declared chemical weapons material and its remaining nuclear materials also has been the subject of scrutiny.[14] NATO officials report that anti- Qadhafi forces now control the sites where key materials of concerns are stored. Libya destroyed the munitions it possessed for dispersing mustard agent in 2004, and since March 2011, U.S. officials have repeatedly stated publicly that they believe the remaining sulfur mustard agent and precursor stockpiles are secure.[15] The now non-weaponized nature of the sulfur mustard agent and precursor materials suggests that they pose a smaller threat than otherwise may have been the case.[16] In late 2010, Libya had restarted the long-delayed destruction of its mustard agent and precursor stockpiles, although technical problems and the outbreak of the conflict resulted in Libya missing its May 2011 deadline for the destruction of its mustard agent. In August 2011, the State Department reported that prior to the conflict, Libya had destroyed over 50% of its mustard agent stocks and over 40% of its liquid chemical weapons precursors. The transitional authorities are expected to reengage with the multilateral Organization for the Prohibition of Chemical Weapons to set a new destruction timetable.

Libya's nuclear materials also have been subject to international and U.S. oversight and joint operations that removed highly enriched uranium and other proliferation-sensitive items. Libya's research reactor east of Tripoli at Tajura was converted with U.S. assistance in 2006 to operate using low-enriched uranium. Libya also possesses a stored stockpile of at least several hundred tons of uranium oxide yellowcake, reportedly stored near the southern contested city of Sebha. Programs to engage Libyan nuclear scientists reportedly have been disrupted by the recent conflict, but may be restarted as the transition unfolds.

Military Support and Disarmament

Throughout the uprising, the United States and its allies debated means for improving the military capabilities and effectiveness of opposition forces while expressing some concern about the identity and intentions of opposition fighters and the proliferation of small arms and heavy weaponry inside Libya and beyond its borders. Some press reports suggest that Qatar provided weaponry to TNC-affiliated forces and that Qatari, British, French, and Jordanian special forces operatives provided military advice to opposition forces, including during the final campaign to seize Tripoli. CRS cannot confirm these reports. The United Kingdom, Italy, and France acknowledged that they had sent military advisers to Benghazi to work to improve opposition command and control arrangements and communications, outside of their governments' support for NATO operations.

U.S. officials have argued that the rebels' most pressing needs are command and control, communications, training, organization, and logistics support. These needs are expected to last beyond the current fighting in addition to emerging needs associated with reconstituting a national military for Libya, incorporating opposition fighters and former regime personnel into security forces, demobilizing civilian volunteers, and destroying excess weaponry and unexploded ordnance. The Administration notified Congress of plan to offer up to $25 million in nonlethal material support to groups in Libya, including the TNC.[17] Deliveries had begun, with roughly half of the authorized amount delivered as of early August 2011.

Libyan Assets, TNC Funding, and Oil Exports

The United States and others froze tens of billions of dollars in Libyan state assets, and the Obama Administration placed targeted sanctions on Libyan oil companies and other entities in support of Executive Order 13566 and the U.N. Security Council resolutions 1970 and 1973. The TNC has identified up to $170 billion in Libyan assets around the world to which it is now seeking access. TNC officials indicate that they plan to prioritize a public financial management assessment in order to give third parties confidence in their ability to responsibly manage blocked assets. U.N. Security Council Resolution 2009 adopted in September 2011 reflects this plan and identifies the World Bank and IMF as partners in conducting the assessment. The intergovernmental Libya Contact Group created a "temporary financial mechanism" to support the TNC,[18] and several governments have pledged hundreds of millions of dollars in aid via this channel.

U.N. Security Council Resolution 2009 reiterated the Security Council's intent to ensure that frozen assets are made available as soon as possible to and for the benefit of the Libyan people:

- The resolution modifies the existing asset freeze requirements related to certain Libyan entities, lifting entirely the measures applicable to the Libyan National Oil Corporation and setting conditions for the release of some frozen assets belonging to the Central Bank of Libya, the Libya Investment Authority, and other prominent national financial entities.

- Under the changes, U.N. member states, after consulting with Libyan authorities, may notify the sanctions committee on Libya of their "intent to authorize access to funds, other financial assets, or economic resources," for five purposes: "humanitarian needs; fuel, electricity and water for strictly civilian uses; resuming Libyan production and sale of hydrocarbons; establishing, operating, or strengthening institutions of civilian government and civilian public infrastructure; or facilitating the resumption of banking sector operations, including to support or facilitate international trade with Libya."
- The Libyan authorities or the U.N. sanctions committee (acting on a consensus basis) may block asset transfer proposals within five days. U.N. asset freezes affecting named individuals remain in place.

Current U.S. Policy on Assets and Sanctions

The Obama Administration has begun transferring $1.5 billion in frozen Libyan assets for the benefit of the Libyan people and the TNC. According to the State Department, the $1.5 billion was identified in consultation with the TNC for the following purposes:[19]

- Transfers to international humanitarian organizations: Up to $120 million for pending United Nations Appeal requests and up to $380 million more for any revised U.N. Appeals for Libya and other humanitarian needs.
- Transfers to suppliers for fuel and other goods for strictly civilian purposes: Up to $500 million to pay for fuel costs for strictly civilian needs (e.g., hospitals, electricity, and desalinization) and for other humanitarian purchases.
- Transfers to the Temporary Financial Mechanism established by the Libya Contact Group: Up to $400 million for providing "key social services, including education and health" and up to $100 million for "food and other humanitarian needs."

The U.S. Department of the Treasury's Office of Foreign Assets Control (OFAC) has issued general licenses, effective September 19, that authorize new transactions with Libyan state entities and maintain the asset freeze established under Executive Order 13566 on named individuals and state entities, with the exception of the National Oil Corporation and other oil sector firms. On September 22, the European Union announced that previously frozen funds belonging to the Central Bank of Libya, the Libyan Investment Authority, the Libyan Foreign Bank, and the Libya Africa Investment Portfolio were authorized to be released "for humanitarian and civilian needs, to support renewed activity in the Libyan oil and banking sectors and to assist with building a civilian government."[20] Resolution 2009 calls on governments to submit individual notifications of intent to the Libyan authorities and the U.N. sanctions committee as part of the process for releasing funds.

Two factors may influence the decisions of U.S. policymakers, their international counterparts, and Libyan authorities about the relative urgency and desirability of releasing frozen funds. First, the TNC's present need for immediate access to blocked assets may be less severe than it appeared in August, given aid and asset transfers to the TNC worth several billion dollars that have taken place since the fall of Tripoli and the changes outlined in Resolution 2009 that facilitate the future sale of oil and the unblocking of some frozen assets. As of late September, open-source estimates suggested that more than $15 billion in blocked Libyan assets had been identified by various governments for transfer to the TNC, and press reports suggested that the TNC had located over $23 billion in previously unknown domestic assets that were contributing to its ability to spend on salaries and services.

Second, countries holding blocked assets, including the United States, may remain wary about the immediate transfer of large sums to the control of the TNC, given emerging political uncertainty about the make-up and priorities of the TNC and its executive authority. Some political groups and local councils are seeking changes to the makeup of the TNC leadership and TNC officials indicate that changes are forthcoming. While recent United Nations resolutions on Libya clearly underscore that blocked assets remain the property of the Libyan people, Resolution 2009 reiterates that, pending transfer for authorized purposes, assets shall remain blocked. It also creates a joint consultation mechanism among Libyan leaders, the sanctions committee, and those governments holding blocked funds.

Libya's Oil Production, Exports, and Revenue

Libya's oil production and export infrastructure appears to have survived the civil conflict relatively unscathed, although some facility damage, the departure of large numbers of laborers and skilled technicians, and the lack of maintenance during the conflict may limit the speed with which production and exports can be restarted.[21] Prior to the conflict, Libya was exporting 1.3

million barrels of oil per day; current production is roughly 60,000 barrels per day. Experts differ in their projections about how soon production and exports could return to pre-conflict levels, with optimistic and pessimistic assumptions differing over expected security conditions, changes to sanctions, and the return of foreign laborers. The importance of oil exports for Libya cannot be overstated, as the IMF reported in February 2011 that over 90% of state revenue came from the hydrocarbon sector in 2010. On September 6, National Oil Company official Nuri Berruien gave an "optimistic forecast" that in 15 months, production would resume at the pre-war level of 1.6 million barrels per day.

Prior to the rebel victory, the U.S. Treasury Department had issued a Statement of Licensing Policy allowing U.S. persons to request from OFAC "specific authorization to trade in hydrocarbon fuel (*i.e.*, oil, gas, and petroleum products) ... to the extent that such hydrocarbon fuel is exported under the auspices of the Transitional National Council of Libya."[22] The license further allowed U.S. persons to request permission "to engage in transactions related to the production of oil, gas, and petroleum products in areas controlled by the Transitional National Council of Libya." More recently released general licenses removed restrictions on transactions with Libyan oil firms.

Humanitarian Conditions and Relief

The gradual consolidation of security and transitional authority control across the country should facilitate greater international humanitarian access to internally displaced Libyans and other communities with humanitarian needs. Those needs are not fully known, but recent assessment visits indicate that the conflict has disrupted the supply of food, medicine, fuel, and other commodities on a nationwide basis. Severe fighting and damage in Sirte and Bani Walid, combined with interruptions to the flow of relief supplies to civilian populations in those areas have been a major concern in recent weeks. The conditional authorization of transfers of assets to and transactions with Libyan government entities could mitigate some concerns about the supply of goods and services to the Libyan population.[23] The TNC, the United Nations, and third parties are expected to discuss needs assessment and resource requirements in more detail over the coming weeks. According to TNC Minister for Reconstruction Jehani, health sector improvements are among the TNC's top priorities because health facilities and personnel have been severely strained and disrupted during the conflict.[24] Secretary of State Hillary Clinton announced the United States plans to offer medical treatment assistance to the Libyan people to help address these challenges.

According to the International Organization for Migration (IOM), as of June 14, over 679,000 people had fled the country since the fighting began.[25] These include Libyans as well as sizable numbers of third country nationals, notably from Sub-Saharan Africa. Throughout the conflict, the U.S. government and its allies have worked to respond to the repatriation and humanitarian needs of third country nationals. It is not clear how many third country nationals and displaced Libyans may seek to return to the country in the immediate aftermath of liberation. Italy and the European Union have expressed concern about the movements of migrants from Libya by sea, in some cases on ships in unsafe conditions. If security and economic conditions improve in Libya, flows of migrants to Europe could slow.

International Criminal Court and United Nations Human Rights Council Investigations[26]

On June 27, 2011, Pre-Trial Chamber I of the International Criminal Court (ICC) issued arrest warrants for three individuals: Muammar al Qadhafi, his son Sayf al Islam al Qadhafi, and intelligence chief Abdullah al Senussi, for "crimes against humanity committed against civilians" not including "war crimes committed during the armed conflict that started at the end of February."[27] ICC Prosecutor Luis Moreno-Ocampo requested the warrants on May 16. On May 4, Moreno-Ocampo reported to the Security Council pursuant to the referral of the situation in Libya since February 15, 2011, to the ICC by Resolution 1970, and stated that the preliminary investigation conducted by the ICC prosecutor's office "establishes reasonable grounds to believe that widespread and systematic attacks against the civilian population, including murder and persecution as crimes against humanity, have been and continue to be committed in Libya," in addition to "war crimes" during the ongoing armed conflict.[28] Prior to Qadhafi's death, some observers argued that the prospect of an ICC trial made it less likely that he would have agreed to relinquish power or to have surrendered to the opposition.[29] Interpol issued arrest warrants for all three individuals. Both the ICC and Interpol have signaled that they intend to maintain their efforts to enforce the warrants against Sayf al Islam al Qadhafi and Abdullah al Senussi, whose whereabouts remain uncertain.

The TNC has been supportive of the ICC efforts to investigate crimes in Libya, but its future plans with regard to the ICC arrest warrants are as yet unclear. TNC officials have pledged to pursue justice for Libyan victims of the recent fighting as well as victims from the Qadhafi era. However, the transfer of individuals to foreign courts could remain politically sensitive for the TNC or its successor. TNC officials have ordered rebel fighters to avoid reprisals, but Qadhafi's death has brought the effectiveness of those orders under increased scrutiny. Some reports suggest that both pro- and anti-Qadhafi forces may have engaged in summary executions during recent fighting in Tripoli, Bani Walid, and Sirte.

On June 1, 2011, the U.N. Human Rights Council's Commission of Inquiry issued a report characterizing the Libyan conflict as "a civil war" and concluded that "international crimes, and specifically crimes against humanity and war crimes, have been committed."[30] With regard to government forces, it stated,

> The commission has found that there have been acts constituting murder, imprisonment, other forms of severe deprivation of physical liberty in violation of fundamental rules of international law, torture, persecution, enforced disappearance and sexual abuse that were committed by Government forces as part of a widespread or systematic attack against a civilian population with knowledge of the attack.... The consistent pattern of violations identified creates an inference that they were carried out as a result of policy decisions by Colonel Qadhafi and members of his inner circle. Further investigation is required in relation to making definitive findings with regard to the identity of those responsible for the crimes committed.

With regard to opposition forces, the commission "established that some acts of torture and cruel treatment and some outrages upon personal dignity in particular humiliating and degrading treatment have been committed by opposition armed forces, in particular against persons in detention, migrant workers and those believed to be mercenaries." These acts could constitute war crimes. The commission "is not of the view that the violations committed by the opposition armed forces were part of any 'widespread or systematic attack' against a civilian population such as to amount to crimes against humanity." The commission considered its findings in light of the future transitional justice needs of the Libyan people and recommended that the U.N. Human Rights Council establish a mechanism to continue the monitoring and investigation of human rights abuses in Libya for a period of one year. Many observers expect that the Council mechanism will investigate the circumstances of Qadhafi's death along with reports of summary executions by both sides of the conflict as part of its monitoring efforts over the coming year.

PROSPECTS AND CHALLENGES FOR U.S. POLICY

Events in Libya remain fluid and fast-moving. After the swell of confidence and international recognition following the capture of Tripoli, Libya's revolutionaries and the TNC now must embark on an uncharted path of political transition and economic recovery. A large number of armed groups are now active and their continued unity of purpose and endorsement of proposed TNC transition plans (see "Interim Transitional National Council (TNC)" below) cannot be taken for granted. Since the uprising began, U.S. officials have argued that U.S. policy must remain flexible in order to effectively shape and respond to changing developments. Given these circumstances, Administration officials and Members of Congress may seek to define U.S. interests; better understand the range of possible outcomes and discuss their potential implications; and define the authorities for and costs of potential U.S. responses in advance.

Some expert observers of Libya's domestic politics have emphasized the general weakness and fractured condition of Libya's political landscape after 40 years of idiosyncratic abuse by Qadhafi and his supporters. Competition among tribal, regional, or political groups that are not now apparent could emerge during any post-conflict negotiations. The political ascendance of nonviolent Islamist opposition forces or the potential intransigence of any of the armed organized factions now active, including armed Islamists, also may create unique challenges. Opposition ranks might split in the short term over differences in opinion about security arrangements or in the long term over the goals and shape of the post-Qadhafi political system. The United States and Europe have expressed concern about violent Islamist groups in Libya and were pursuing counterterrorism cooperation with the Qadhafi government prior to the unrest.

Possible Questions

Possible questions that Members of Congress may wish to consider when assessing the recent developments in Libya and proposals regarding continued U.S. military operations, foreign assistance, or political engagement in Libya include the following:

- In the wake of Qadhafi's downfall, what are the goals of U.S. policy in Libya? What U.S. national interests are at stake? What options exist for securing them? How might continued U.S. or multilateral military interventions to protect civilians contribute to or detract from those goals? What advisory support and assistance should be provided to interim authorities via military and civilian means?
- How are events in Libya likely to shape developments in the broader Middle East and North Africa? What unintended consequences may result from regime change in Libya? What opportunities does regime change present? What precedents have U.S. or multilateral military intervention in the Libyan conflict set and how might those precedents affect the context in which U.S. decision makers respond to other regional crises and events?
- When should the United States transfer Libyan assets to a new Libyan governing authority and for what purposes? Should the United States seek reimbursement from Libya for the cost of military operations or humanitarian assistance?
- In addition to UNSMIL, which actors are providing assistance and advice to Libyans on security, stabilization, and reconstruction in the wake of the conflict? Under what authority and on what terms? What role, if any, will the United States play in a post-conflict setting? What appropriations or authorizations might be required to support such a role?
- Which individuals and groups are emerging as key political, economic, and security actors in Libya? What are their relative goals and agendas? What should be the key components of a future U.S.-Libyan bilateral relationship? What limits to engagement, if any, should the United States impose on its dealings with different Libyan groups? What type of security relationship, if any, should the United States pursue with a new Libyan government?
- What steps, if any, should the United States take to assist Libyan authorities in securing chemical weapons stockpiles and nuclear

materials? What can and should be done to limit the proliferation of conventional weaponry within and beyond Libya?

LIBYAN POLITICAL DYNAMICS AND PROFILES

Political Dynamics

Prior to the recent conflict, Libya's political dynamics were characterized by competition among interest groups seeking to influence policy within the confines of the country's authoritarian political system and amid Libya's emergence from international isolation. Economic reformers embraced changes to Libya's former socialist model to meet current needs, even as political reforms languished amid disputes between hard-line political forces and reform advocates. In general, the legacies of Italian colonial occupation and Libya's struggle for independence in the early-to-mid-20th century continue to influence Libyan politics. This is reflected in the celebration of the legacy of the anti-colonial figure Omar al Mukhtar during the current uprising.

Prior to the recent unrest, rhetorical references to preserving sovereignty and resistance to foreign domination were common in political statements from all parties. Wariness of ground-based foreign intervention and the slogan "Libyans can do it on their own" common among Libyans reflect that sentiment and are likely to persist in a post-Qadhafi environment. Most Libyans accept a prominent role for Islamic tradition in public life, but differ in their personal preferences and interpretations of their faith. Islam is the official religion and the Quran is the nominal basis for the country's law and its social code.

Tribal relationships have remained socially important, particularly in non-urban settings, and had some political role under Qadhafi with regard to the distribution of leadership positions in government ministries, in some economic relationships between some social groups and families, and in political-military relations. Tribal loyalties reportedly remain strong within and between branches of the armed services, and members of Qadhafi's tribe, the Qadhafa, have held many high-ranking government positions. Some members of larger tribes, such as the Magariha, Misurata, and the Warfalla, sought to advance their broad interests under Qadhafi through control of official positions of influence, although some of their members opposed the regime on grounds of tribal discrimination.

Competition for influence among Libya's regions characterized the pre-Qadhafi period, and some saw the 1969 Qadhafi-led revolution as having been partly facilitated by western and southern Libyan resentments of the Al Sanusi monarchy based in the eastern Libyan region of Cyrenaica. More recent Libyan politics have not been dominated by overt inter-regional tension, although pro-Qadhafi forces accused the organizers and leaders of the revolt as having, inter alia, an eastern regional separatist agenda. The TNC denied these accusations and has quickly moved representatives westward to Tripoli, while proposing changes to the structure and membership of the TNC to improve national representation. Some reports suggest that federalism is one model being explored by some groups, although the TNC has not endorsed federalism to date.

Political parties and all opposition groups were banned under Qadhafi. Formal political pluralism was frowned upon by many members of the ruling elite, even as, in the period preceding the unrest, some regime figures advocated for greater popular participation in existing government institutions. The general lack of widespread experience in formal political organization, competition, and administration is likely to remain a challenge in the immediate post-Qadhafi era. Independent NGO reports suggest ad hoc political organization is ongoing across opposition-held areas and much of it reflects a desire for institution-based, democratic governance rooted in the rule of law. Some nascent political and social groups have sought external training and support to overcome the legacy of decades of restrictions. The continued openness of newly liberated Libyans to outside examples and assistance remains to be determined, and different groups are likely to take different approaches.

Prior to the 2011 uprising, Libya's opposition movements were often categorized broadly as Islamist, royalist, or secular nationalist in orientation. Their activities and effectiveness had been largely limited by government repression and infiltration, disorganization, rivalry, and ideological differences. New efforts to coordinate opposition activities had begun in response to Libya's reintegration to the international community and the emergence of a broader political reform debate in the Arab world, and gained momentum with the outbreak of region-wide protests and political change in late 2010 and early 2011. The infusion of popular support and regime defectors to the broadly defined opposition cause inside Libya was welcomed by many established opposition groups, even if the specific political demands of newly active opposition supporters and their compatibility with the agendas of the established groups remain unclear.

The emergence of real political competition during Libya's post-conflict and post-authoritarian transition creates unique challenges for U.S. policymakers, among which are identifying new leaders and groups; determining their relative intentions, goals, and legitimacy; and assessing the capabilities and intentions of armed elements.

Interim Transitional National Council (TNC)

Early in the uprising against Qadhafi, opposition leaders formed a 45-member Interim Transitional National Council (TNC) in the eastern city of Benghazi to coordinate resistance efforts and to serve as an international representative for the Libyan people. Endorsements from self-organized local councils established some basic political legitimacy and authority for the TNC, and its leaders addressed their plans and appeals to all Libyans regardless of region or political orientation in the hopes of maintaining unity. The TNC took on some of the functions of government in liberated areas of the east, although all accounts suggest that Libyan citizens' volunteer efforts and restraint were mainly responsible for the maintenance of order. The TNC's authority over volunteer fighters appeared tenuous at best during much of the conflict.

As of late October, the TNC had assumed responsibility for transition efforts nationwide, working through the local councils that established its legitimacy. Leading TNC figures have relocated to Tripoli to direct efforts from the capital. Many world governments have recognized the TNC as "the legitimate representative of the Libyan people," and the U.N. General Assembly voted to grant the TNC Libya's seat at the United Nations. The United States government refers to the TNC as "the legitimate interlocutor for the Libyan people during this interim period."

Throughout the conflict, limited information has been available about the TNC's relationships with many emergent opposition leaders, particularly in western Libya, whose identities TNC leaders claimed needed to remain secret for their protection. The prominent role played by western activists and armed elements in capturing Tripoli and the criticism that some groups have made of TNC leaders and decisions in the wake of the capture of Tripoli illustrates the challenges facing the TNC. Some opposition supporters, including the Libyan Muslim Brotherhood and local leaders from Misuratah, have indicated they will not support the participation of some former government officials in any future transitional political arrangement. These concerns led to delays in announcing a reorganization of the TNC executive authority and may now delay the formation of an interim government, even though critical groups and figures have endorsed the TNC's transition roadmap in general terms.

The TNC has laid out key aspects of its political platform and proposed roadmap for the transition in a bid to communicate clearly with domestic supporters and the international community. The TNC also has taken steps to clarify the legislative role of the Council and the role of its "executive authority" and "stabilization team."

- According to TNC officials and a draft interim national charter, current plans call for local councils to select representatives to a reconstituted National Transitional Council, which will remain "the supreme authority" in Libya, deriving its legitimacy from "the Revolution of February 17."[31] A declaration of liberation will has started the proposed sequence for the transition, with key milestones expected over a period of 20 months.
- After naming an interim government—within 30 days of a declaration of liberation—the TNC is to choose members by secret ballot for a Constitutional Authority to draft a constitution that would then be subject to a popular referendum. Within 60 days of the approval of a constitution, the TNC will provide electoral laws for U.N.-supervised national elections to be held within six months for a legislature and president.
- The executive authority, which has been led by Prime Minister Mahmoud Jibril and deputy chairman Ali Tarhouni, plays a cabinet function. Individuals are responsible for discrete portfolios including internal security, foreign relations, social affairs, reconstruction and Islamic endowments, among others. Jibril has announced his intention to resign, and it appears likely that Tarhouni will take a leading role until the interim government is formed.
- The stabilization team, led by Minister for Reconstruction Ahmed Jehani, is responsible for overseeing transition efforts across all sectors. The team developed detailed plans in consultation with Libyans and external parties in preparation for the end of the conflict. Minister Jehani is now coordinating TNC interaction with external parties on implementing those plans in key sectors such as public finance, public security, health, education, and civil service reform.

Transition plans include a series of restrictions on the ability of TNC and executive authority members from holding dual office, benefitting from transactions involving state property, and standing for some future elected positions. The draft charter states that "Islam is the religion of the state and the principal source of legislation is Islamic jurisprudence (*sharia*).... The State shall guarantee for non-Moslems the freedom of practicing religious rights and shall guarantee respect for their systems of personal status."

Prominent TNC Figures

- **Mustafa Abdeljalil.** (aka Mustafa Abdeljalil Fadl) Serves as chairman of the interim Transitional National Council. He served as Libya's justice minister from 2007 through the onset of the uprising. He is known for having been supportive of some reform initiatives advanced by Sayf al Islam al Qadhafi and for challenging Muammar al Qadhafi and his supporters regarding due process and incarceration of prisoners in some prominent legal cases during 2009 and 2010. He attempted to resign from his position in early 2010.[32] He is a native of Bayda, where he once served as chief judge. He is 59 years old. In February, Abdeljalil claimed to have evidence that Qadhafi ordered the terrorist attack on Pan Am Flight 103. His statements suggest he is sympathetic to demands from Islamist groups that their interests be reflected in transitional arrangements.
- **Mahmoud Jibril.** (aka Mahmoud Jibril Ibrahim Al Warfali) Mahmoud Jibril has served as the interim prime minister and the foreign affairs representative for the executive bureau of the TNC since its formation. He has recently expressed his intention to resign, citing opposition to his continued service from a range of domestic interest groups, many of which have made public statements questioning his performance. He is a graduate of the University of Pittsburgh, where he earned a masters degree in political science and a Ph.D. in planning in the early 1980s. He is 58 years old, and is described by personal acquaintances and professional contacts as being intelligent, moderate, analytical, detail-oriented, and an articulate English speaker. He worked as an independent consultant prior to serving as the secretary of the Libyan National Planning Council and director-general of the National Economic Development Board (NEDB) from 2007 onward. The NEDB was a government entity affiliated with Muammar al Qadhafi's relatively reform-oriented son Sayf al Islam that was tasked with proposing institutional reform and attracting foreign investment and educational exchange opportunities to Libya. He visited Washington, DC, during the week of May 9 and met with Members of Congress, Senators, and Administration officials.

- **Ali Tarhouni.** Served as the vice chairman of the TNC executive authority and its primary oil and finance representative until the position of vice chairman was eliminated in the October 2011 reorganization of the executive authority. He retained his finance and oil portfolio and remains active in TNC efforts to implement transition plans. He returned to Libya from the United States where he has lived since the early 1970s and worked as an economics professor at the University of Washington.
- **Abdel Hafez Ghoga**. Serves as a spokesman for the TNC. He is described in the Libyan press as a "human rights lawyer and community organizer." Reports suggest that Ghoga had been working to organize a national transitional council at the same time as Mustafa Abdeljalil and others were working to form the TNC. The two figures reportedly agreed to cooperate.
- **Ahmed Jehani.** Serves as minister of infrastructure and reconstruction and chairman of the TNC "stabilization team." Jehani is a former World Bank adviser and country director. He served with Mahmoud Jibril as the associate director general of the National Economic Development Board (NEDB). In the 1970s he served as general counsel for the Libyan National Oil Company. He holds legal degrees from Harvard and the Fletcher School of Law and Diplomacy.

Armed Forces

The TNC and volunteer militia groups established a military council to coordinate the efforts of volunteers and defectors, and a Tripoli-based higher security council seeks to coordinate the efforts of volunteer militia groups and former regime security officials. TNC representatives have sought to manage rivalries among leading defectors, former exiles, and volunteers, while remaining vague about the role of former regime military forces who defected. Rebel operations during the conflict do not appear to have featured intact regular military units. Opposition-affiliated forces include the "17 February Forces," the "Army of Free Libya," and groups made up of various volunteers, including secularists and Islamists. City-based militias remain active and have demonstrated a willingness and ability to work independently of their counterparts and the TNC.

Consistent coordination among the different volunteer armed elements has not been apparent, and key figures Abdelfattah Younis al Ubaydi and Khalifah Belqasim Haftar reportedly competed for leadership of the opposition's overall efforts prior to Younis's assassination in July by an unidentified faction.[33]

During the conflict, much of the reporting from combat areas regularly described the opposition as mostly untrained, poorly equipped, uncoordinated, and without professional logistics or communications support.[34] The coordinated assault on Tripoli, including the reported intervention by Misuratah-based fighters, appeared to belie those descriptions and suggest improvement, even as subsequent urban fighting in Tripoli and in pro-Qadhafi strongholds in Sirte, Bani Walid, and Sebha was chaotic.

At present, prominent military and security figures include

- **Major General Jalal al Dughayli.** Renamed as the military affairs chief (or "defense minister") of the TNC executive authority in October 2011. Visited Egypt and Qatar in his capacity as defense chief for the TNC during conflict. In his address following Qadhafi's death, he urged volunteer fighters to obey TNC authorities and direct their weapons and vehicles for the use of the new Libyan armed forces. He also urged Libyans to turn from the "lesser jihad" of combat to the "greater jihad" of a building "a modern homeland based on the constitution, law, party pluralism, justice, democracy, and freedom."[35]
- **Omar al Hariri**. Served as a military affairs representative on the TNC prior to October 2011. Hariri participated in 1969 anti-monarchy coup alongside Qadhafi, but later was imprisoned and sentenced to death on suspicion of plotting an uprising in 1975. He was moved to Tobruk and placed under house arrest in 1990. He is 67 years old. He has been quoted as calling for "a multi-party system" for Libya.
- **Abdelfattah Younis al Ubaydi**. Assassinated in July 2011. Participated in the 1969 anti-monarchy coup alongside Qadhafi. Prior to the conflict, he served as minister for public security and a special forces commander, which put him in charge of some internal security forces through the start of the uprising. His resignation and defection came just hours after Muammar al Qadhafi specifically named him as one of his key supporters in a February 22 speech. Human rights concerns prior to and potentially during the beginning of the unrest could have involved forces under his command. He was the TNC-appointed leader of military operations and remained an outspoken advocate for the opposition cause until his death. Subsequent reports suggested that allegations that he misled the opposition about his activities and forces may have contributed to suspicions that he remained a clandestine Qadhafi supporter.

- **Colonel Khalifah Belqasim Haftar**. A veteran of the ill-fated Libyan invasion of Chad during the 1980s, he turned against Qadhafi. Colonel Haftar returned to Libya from exile in the United States after the uprising began.[36] In the past, Haftar has been mentioned as a leader of the Libyan Movement for Change and Reform and the Libyan National Army, an armed opposition group reported to have received support from foreign intelligence agencies and alleged to have been involved in past attempts to overthrow Qadhafi.[37] Press reports suggest Haftar is contributing to training and command efforts and either took or was granted the rank/title of general. Reports also suggest that the TNC may have sought to remove him from a command role, and that Haftar has resisted those efforts.
- **Major Abdelmoneim Al Huni**. An original member of the Revolution Command Council, Al Huni had been serving as Libya's representative to the Arab League and resigned in protest of the use of force against protestors. Regional press accounts from the 1990s describe Al Huni as having coordinated with the opposition efforts of Colonel Haftar and others, before Al Huni reconciled with Qadhafi in 2000.
- **Abdelhakim Belhajj**. Reported to be the commander of a significant contingent of opposition forces involved in the capture of Tripoli, Belhajj is otherwise known as the former commander of the Libyan Islamic Fighting Group, a U.S.- designated Foreign Terrorist Organization. Belhajj, a veteran of the anti-Soviet period in Afghanistan, fled Afghanistan via Iran and Thailand in the wake of the U.S. invasion in 2001 and was detained and transferred to Libyan detention. He remained imprisoned until 2010, when he was released as part of a reconciliation agreement between the Qadhafi government and the LIFG.[38]
- **Abdullah Ahmed Nakir al Zintani.** Chairman of the Tripoli Council of Revolutionaries, whose armed wing has been reported to include up to 7,000 armed fighters. In September he told an interviewer, “"We fought and brought down Al Qadhafi's regime. We fought the battle for ours and our people's freedom. No new government can be formed without our knowledge, and we must be represented in it. ... We have cadres of seasoned politicians and even academics of the highest level, who should join the government. We should get 50 percent of the ministerial portfolios.”[39]

Exiles and Al Sanusi Monarchy Figures

Complex relationships among former regime figures, competing heirs to the former monarchy (1951-1969), and long-standing opposition leaders may evolve as specific arrangements are made for reconciliation and a new government.

Opposition groups in exile have included the National Alliance, the Libyan National Movement (LNM), the Libyan Movement for Change and Reform, the Islamist Rally, the National Libyan Salvation Front (NLSF), and the Republican Rally for Democracy and Justice. These groups and others held an opposition conference—known as the National Conference for the Libyan Opposition (NCLO)—in July 2005 in London and issued a "national accord," calling for the removal of Qadhafi from power and the establishment of a transitional government.[40] A follow-up meeting was held in March 2008.[41] The NCLO reportedly helped lead the call for the February 17, 2011, "day of rage" that helped catalyze protests into a full-blown uprising against Qadhafi.

A royalist contingent based on the widely recognized claim to the leadership of the royal family by Mohammed al Rida al Sanusi, the son of the former Libyan crown prince, has been based in London.[42] His claim is disputed by a distant relative, whose family members also have given interviews to international media outlets. On April 20, Mohammed al Sanusi met with members of the European Parliament and said, "it is up to the Libyan people to decide whether they go down the road of a constitutional monarchy or that of a republic." He recently repeated similar sentiments and called on Libyans "to lay the foundations for a democratic state." The Libyan constitutional monarchy system was overturned by Qadhafi in 1969, and Al Sanusi believes the old constitution, if "suitably updated," could "form the basis of a new Libya." He also has pledged to "assist in creating a democratic state for Libyans based on a representative parliament chosen by free and fair elections."

Libyan Islamists and the TNC

Like citizens in other Middle Eastern societies, Libyans have grappled with questions posed by Islamist activism, state repression of Islamist groups, and violent Islamist extremism over a period of decades. As the transition period unfolds, Libyans will be debating the role of Islamist groups in political life, the role of Islam in society, and the nature and proper responses to threats posed by armed extremist groups. These debates may have implications for U.S. policy toward Libya and the region.

The Muslim Brotherhood

A statement attributed to the Libyan Muslim Brotherhood in late February 2011 welcomed the formation of the TNC but called for a future, non-tribal government to "be formed by those who actually led the revolution on the ground" and to exclude supporters of the original Qadhafi coup or officials involved in human rights violations.[43] This would seem to implicate some original Qadhafi allies and security officials who have defected to the opposition cause. An individual with reported links to the Muslim Brotherhood, Dr. Ali al Salabi, has criticized the TNC leadership on these grounds in the wake of the capture of Tripoli.[44] In the past, the controller general of the Libyan Muslim Brotherhood, Suleiman Abdel Qadir, has described the Brotherhood's objectives as peaceful and policy-focused, and has long called for the cancellation of laws restricting political rights.[45] In a September interview, he reportedly stated "I think it is wrong to describe some revolutionaries as extremists because this could trigger dire reaction. It is also wrong to talk of benefitting from the cadres of the [former Libyan] regime in the forthcoming stage."[46]

Like other political organizations and opposition groups, the Muslim Brotherhood was banned in Libya under Qadhafi. Since the late 1940s, when members of the Egyptian Muslim Brotherhood first entered Libya following a crackdown on their activities, the Libyan Muslim Brotherhood has existed as a semi-official organization. Hundreds of Brotherhood members and activists were jailed in 1973, although the Brotherhood eventually reemerged and operated as a clandestine organization for much of the following two decades. In 1998, a second round of mass arrests took place, and 152 Brotherhood leaders and members were arrested. Several reportedly died in custody, and, following trials in 2001 and 2002, two prominent Brotherhood leaders were sentenced to death and over 70 were sentenced to life in prison.[47] The government announced a retrial for the imprisoned Brotherhood activists in October 2005, and in March 2006, the group's 84 remaining imprisoned members were released.[48]

Libyan Islamic Fighting Group (LIFG)/Libyan Islamic Movement for Change (LIMC)

The LIFG is a U.S.-designated Foreign Terrorist Organization and Islamist movement that used violence in past attempts to overthrow Muammar al Qadhafi and his government.[49] Over the last 20-plus years, members of the LIFG are reported to have fought in various conflicts around the world involving Muslims, including in Afghanistan during the 1980s, the Balkans during the 1990s, and Iraq after 2003. According to the U.S. State Department, members of the group at times have demonstrated distinct and competing priorities: "some members maintained a strictly anti-Qadhafi focus ... others ... aligned with Osama bin Laden, and are believed to be part of the Al Qaeda leadership structure or active in international terrorism."[50] According to the 2010 State Department report on terrorism released in August 2011, many LIFG members in Europe and Libya rejected a 2007 statement by Ayman al Zawahiri and the late Abu Layth Al Libi announcing the merger of the LIFG with Al Qaeda.[51] In a July 2009 statement, LIFG members in Britain characterized the November 2007 Al Qaeda affiliation announcement as "a personal decision that is at variance with the basic status of the group," and sought to "clearly emphasize that the group is not, has never been, and will never be, linked to the Al Qaeda organization."[52]

While publicly rejecting Al Qaeda affiliation, the 2009 LIFG statement warned the Qadhafi government that the group would "preserve [its] lawful and natural right to oppose the regime if it does not turn its back on its previous policy that has led to tension and deadlock." The participation of LIFG figures in recent military operations against pro-Qadhafi forces illustrated this commitment. However, prior to the recent unrest, many leading LIFG figures had been imprisoned and released after renouncing the use of violence as part of a dialogue and reconciliation process with the Qadhafi government.[53] Some figures affiliated with the LIFG, such as current Tripoli-based militia commander Abdelhakim Belhajj, participated in this reconciliation process and have reiterated their rejection of Al Qaeda and its ideology in public interviews in recent weeks (see below).

Some Libya-based members of the LIFG responded to the release of leading figures on February 16 by announcing the reorganization of the group as the Libyan Islamic Movement for Change (LIMC). The LIMC demands political change and an end to corruption, and has underscored its decision to "enter a new stage of struggle in which we do not adopt an armed program but a belief in the Libyan people's ability to bring about the change to which we are aspiring."[54]

Al Qaeda Affiliation and Recantations

The United States froze the LIFG's U.S. assets under Executive Order 13224 in September 2001, and formally designated the LIFG as a Foreign

Terrorist Organization in December 2004. In February 2006, the U.S. Department of the Treasury designated five individuals and four entities in the United Kingdom as Specially Designated Global Terrorists for their role in supporting the LIFG.[55] On October 30, 2008, Treasury designated three more LIFG financiers.[56] Some observers characterized the designations as a U.S. gesture of solidarity with the Qadhafi government and argued that the ability and willingness of the LIFG to mount terror attacks in Libya may have been limited. Others claimed that some LIFG fighters were allied with other violent Islamist groups operating in the trans-Sahara region, and cited evidence of Libyan fighters joining the Iraqi insurgency as an indication of ongoing Islamist militancy in Libya and a harbinger of a possible increase in violence associated with fighters returning from Iraq.[57]

In November 2007, Al Qaeda figures Ayman al Zawahiri and Abu Layth al Libi announced the merger of the LIFG with Al Qaeda, which many terrorism analysts viewed at the time as having political rather than operational relevance.[58] Abu Layth Al Libi was killed in an air strike in Pakistan in February 2008. The group's reported ties with Al Qaeda came under scrutiny in July 2009 after group members based in Britain reportedly renounced the group's affiliation with Al Qaeda, and contrasted the LIFG with others who use indiscriminate bombing and target civilians.[59] The statement warned that the group would "preserve [its] lawful and natural right to oppose the regime if it does not turn its back on its previous policy that has led to tension and deadlock."

The Libyan government and the LIFG reached an agreement in which LIFG leaders renounced violence against the Libyan state, and, later in 2009, the dialogue resulted in the issuance of written "recantations" of the LIFG's former views on religion and violence.[60] In October 2009, over 40 LIFG prisoners were released, alongside other Islamists. However, Libyan and U.S. concerns about LIFG's domestic and international activities persisted. Qadhafi announced the release of the final 110 "reconciled" LIFG members at the outset of the 2011 uprising, reportedly including Abdelwahhab Muhammad Qayid, who has been identified in some sources as the brother of prominent Al Qaeda ideologue Abu Yahya al Libi. In March 2011, Abu Yahya Al Libi released a video condemning Qadhafi and calling on Libyans to use arms against Qadhafi supporters, but to refrain from violence or criminality against each other.[61]

Al Qaeda in the Lands of the Islamic Maghreb (AQLIM/AQIM)[62]

U.S. government officials and their regional counterparts remain focused on the potential for the unrest in Libya to provide opportunities to Al Qaeda's regional affiliate, Al Qaeda in the Lands of the Islamic Maghreb (AQLIM/AQIM). Some press reports suggest that AQIM personnel have obtained weaponry from looted Libyan military stockpiles, including surface-to-air missiles. The Algerian, Malian, and Chadian governments continue to express concern about the potential for instability in Libya to weaken security along Libya's long borders, which could allow AQIM operatives and criminal networks that provide services to AQIM to move more freely.

While the imprisoned, Libya-based leaders of the LIFG participated in reconciliation with Qadhafi's government and renounced violence as a domestic political tool, the participation of some of their supporters in efforts to send Libyans abroad to participate in insurgencies and terrorism has raised concerns about the potential for cooperation between AQIM and some Libyan Islamists. Former Guantanamo Bay detainee Abu Sufian Hamuda Bin Qumu has attracted some media attention, and one figure, Abdelhakim Al Hasadi, is leading ad hoc security arrangements in the eastern city of Darnah, which was home to several dozen Libyan recruits who travelled to Iraq to fight U.S. and coalition forces.[63] TNC oversight of his operations is not apparent, although he has indicated his support for the Council's role. As noted above, the group's former commander, Abdelhakim Belhajj, is playing a leadership role in some military operations in and around Tripoli. Some Libyan observers have been critical of international media coverage of these individuals and argue they represent an exception and have been given too much attention.

On April 16, London-based pan-Arab newspaper *Al Hayat* published an email interview with a reported spokesman for AQIM named Salah Abu Muhammad, who stated that AQIM had obtained weaponry from Libyan military stockpiles and claimed that AQIM had cooperative relationships with Al Hasadi and so-called "emirates" in several eastern Libyan cities. A subsequent statement from another reported AQIM source accused Algerian intelligence services of fabricating the Abu Muhammad interview.[64] Neither source could be independently verified.

A March 17 statement attributed to AQIM leader Abdelmalik Droukdel (aka Abu Mus'ab al Wudud) addressed Libyan rebels and sought to associate the Libyan uprising with Al Qaeda's campaign against Arab and Western governments.[65] The statement advised Libyans to avoid cooperation with the United States and "to rally around the revolutionary leaders who are holding fast to their Islamic faith and whose readiness to make sacrifices has been proven on the battlefield." Other AQIM figures have sought to explain that their organization is not seeking to direct or claim credit for the Libyan uprising, but that AQIM is supportive of the campaign against Qadhafi.

Transitional National Council Positions and Statements

To date, the leadership of the TNC has not demonstrated rhetorical or material support for Al Qaeda, the Muslim Brotherhood, or Hamas. TNC officials repeatedly emphasize their concerns about the proliferation of small arms and light weapons within and potentially beyond Libya. The TNC has not taken public positions on a number of foreign policy matters—including the Israeli-Palestinian conflict—in line with its commitment to leave the definition of Libyan foreign policy to a future elected government. On March 30, the TNC released a statement affirming its support for U.N. Security Council resolutions on Al Qaeda and the Taliban and U.N. conventions on terrorism. The statement "affirms the Islamic identity of the Libyan People, its commitment to the moderate Islamic values, its full rejection to the extremist ideas and its commitment to combating them in all circumstances, and refuses the allegations aiming to associate al-Qaeda with the revolutionists in Libya."

Since the capture of Tripoli, TNC leaders have reemphasized their rejection of ideological extremism among Libyans and are seeking to unite different interest groups for the transition period. As noted above, the TNC's draft interim constitutional charter, released in August, states in Article One that "Libya is an independent Democratic State wherein the people are the source of authorities.... Islam is the Religion of the State and the principal source of legislation is Islamic Jurisprudence (*sharia*).... The State shall guarantee for non-Muslims the freedom of practicing religious rights and shall guarantee respect for their systems of personal status." On September 12, TNC Chairman Mustafa Abdeljalil said in a public address in Tripoli that the TNC is "seeking to establish the rule of law, a welfare state, and a state in which Islamic sharia will be the main source of legislation.... we will not allow any extremist ideology, whether on the left or on the right. We are a Muslim people, our Islam is moderate, and we will preserve that."[66]

TNC officials have continuously denied that their ranks or those of their military supporters include Al Qaeda operatives, although some TNC officials have made statements expressing concern that extremist groups are active in Libya and may seek to exploit the recent fighting and transition. For example:

- On August 22, Chairman Abdeljalil told an *Al Jazeera* interviewer that he "was planning to resign from the council the day Abd-al-

Fattah Yunus [former commander of Libyan rebels] was killed as long as the rebels think in such a manner. It does not honor me to work for a council that oversees rebels with such mentality. We have some extremist Islamists.... I tell you candidly that there are extremist Islamist groups that seek to have revenge and to create turbulence in the Libyan society. I will not be honored to be the head of a National Transitional Council with such rebels working for it."[67] Subsequent reports suggest that TNC officials have identified and detained the individuals suspected of involvement in the murder of Yunus. TNC officials have not confirmed the ideological affiliation of those individuals, and a trial is expected.

- On August 28, TNC military commander Khalifah Heftar said in an *Al Arabiya* television interview: "I was asked before whether Al Qaeda elements have joined us. I answered this question by saying that had there been Al Qaeda groups here in Libya, I would not have been in this position. However, I knew that there are extremist groups in Libya, and this extremism does not lie in the interest of the Libyan people, and I do not think the Libyan people accept this extremism."[68]

U.S. and regional observers continue to closely monitor statements from and actions by AQIM, Libyan Islamists, and the TNC.

End Notes

[1] On October 23, NATO Secretary-General Anders Fogh-Rassmussen said, "Our NATO-led operation to protect the people of Libya, under the historic mandate of the United Nations, is very close to completion. We have taken a preliminary decision to end Operation Unified Protector on October 31, and we will take a formal decision in the next few days." "Statement by the NATO Secretary-General on the Liberation of Libya, October 23, 2011.

[2] As of September 8, rebels from Zintan under the command of the Madani clan claimed to have 5,000 armed men in Tripoli. Fighters from Misuratah reportedly shifted toward the pursuit of pro-Qadhafi forces in Sirte and Bani Walid and their numbers in Tripoli had declined to 1,500. Belhajj claims to have taken a leading role in the Tripoli operations. He was released from prison by the Qadhafi government in 2010 as part of a reconciliation agreement with LIFG fighters in exchange for their renunciation of violence. See Adrien Jaulmes, "The Fragile Patchwork of the Libyan Rebels," *Le Figaro* (Paris), September 8, 2011; U.S. Open Source Center (OSC) Report GMP20110824715001, "Rebel Commander Balhaj Urges Al-Qadhafi Brigades To 'Abandon' Regime," August 20, 2011; and OSC Report GMP20100323950045, "Three Leaders of Libyan Fighting Group Freed – Paper," March 23, 2010.

[3] OSC Report GMP20111023001007, "Libya: TNC Chairman Mustafa Abd-al-Jalil on Aftermath of Al-Qadhafi's Death," October 23, 2011.

[4] Overview of United States Activities in Libya, June 15, 2011. Available from CRS.

[5] Remarks by TNC Minister for Reconstruction Ahmed Jehani and U.S. Ambassador to Libya Gene Cretz.

[6] CRS cannot independently verify the state of the opposition's finances, but one opposition source indicated that, as of May, costs had reached $100 million per day, with gasoline and other fuel imports constituting a particularly critical need. Richard Spencer and Ruth Sherlock, "Libya's Rebels To Run Out of Money 'in Three Weeks,'" *Telegraph* (UK), May 3, 2011; VOA News, "Libya's Rebel Envoy Seeks Frozen Assets," August 25, 2011.

[7] CRS interviews and review of unpublished NGO and unclassified State Department reporting, May and September 2011.

[8] The United Nations Department of Political Affairs is responsible for UNSMIL and is funded through assessed contributions of U.N. member states, including the United States.

[9] For example, these concerns were raised in C. J. Chivers, "Experts Fear Looted Libyan Arms May Find Way to Terrorists," *New York Times*, March 3, 2011. African Union communiqués have expressed concern about regional stability, and some Sahel region governments have specifically warned about Al Qaeda supporters seizing control of specific types of weapons and exploiting the weakness of government forces in Libya to expand their areas of operation and sanctuary. Algerian authorities have reportedly expanded the presence of security forces along their border with Libya and have announced operations to eliminate weapons smugglers and seize smuggled weaponry and explosives.

[10] The notification requirements were waived pursuant to Section 634a of the Foreign Assistance Act of 1961 and Sections 7015(f) and 7015 (e) of the Department of State, Foreign Operations, and Related Programs Appropriations Act (SFOAA), 2010 (Div. F, P.L. 111-117), as amended and carried forward by the Full-Year Continuing Appropriations Act, 2011 (Div. B, P.L. 112-10). The notification states, "The fighting in Libya and NATO air strikes have left many ammunition storage areas totally unsecured and open to looting.... There is little or no perimeter security at the storage sites, and munitions and small arms and light weapons, including thousands of MANPADS, have been looted for weeks. It is critically important not only to the Libyan population, but to counter the threat of proliferation into neighboring regions that work begin immediately to collect, control, and destroy conventional weapons and munitions, and reestablish security at these storage sites. Terrorist groups are exploiting this opportunity and the situation grows more dangerous with each passing day, a situation that directly impacts U.S. national security."

[11] For more information see the United Nations Mine Action Service website at http://www.mineaction.org/ overview.asp?o=3994.

[12] Reuters, "Israel sees Libya as New Source of Arms for Gaza," July 21, 2011.

[13] Reuters, "Israel Says Gaza Gets Anti-Plane Arms from Libya," August 29, 2011.

[14] For an overview of Libya's declared chemical weapons and nuclear materials see U.S. State Department, *Condition (10) (C) Report - Compliance with the Convention on the Prohibition of the Development, Production, Stockpiling and Use of Chemical Weapons and on their Destruction*, August 2011; and, International Atomic Energy Agency (IAEA) Board of Governors, *Implementation of the NPT Safeguards Agreement in the Socialist People's Libyan Arab Jamahiriya*, GOV/2008/39, September 12, 2008.

[15] The chemical materials are stored at Rabta, southwest of Tripoli and Ruwagha, near the Al Jufrah Air Force Base in central Libya. According to the U.S. State Department, identified mustard and nerve agent precursors present in Libya included pinacolyl alcohol,

isopropanol, phosphorus trichloride, 2-chloroethanol, tributylamine, and thionyl chloride. See State Department, Office of the Spokesperson, "Libya: Securing Stockpiles Promotes Security," August 26, 2011.

[16] "We believe that it's secure," said Colonel David Lapan, a Pentagon spokesman. "Even if not weaponized, there's still a threat, but it's a smaller threat than if it is weaponized." Agence France Presse, "Libya Has Mustard Gas, Lacks Delivery Systems: Monitor," March 10, 2011.

[17] Items have been drawn from Defense Department stocks and may include medical first aid kits, stretchers, bandages & dressing, surgical tape, blankets, meals ready to eat, tents, sleeping bags, canteens, uniforms, boots, tactical load-bearing vests, bullet-proof vests, military helmets, maps, binoculars, infrared markers, panel marker, infrared (glint) tape, HESCOS (or sandbags), hand shovels, and 9 volt batteries. CRS communication with State Department, April 29, 2011.

[18] Over 20 Contact Group members attended the meeting in Rome including and officials from the Arab League, the African Union, the World Bank, NATO, the Gulf Cooperation Council (GCC), the Organization of the Islamic Conference (OIC), the United Arab Emirates (UAE), Australia, Bahrain, Denmark, France, Germany, Greece, Jordan, Morocco, Netherland, Poland, Romania, Malta, Canada, Tunisia, Spain, Turkey, the United Kingdom, the United States, Sudan and the Holy See. Portugal observed the meeting.

[19] State Department, Office of the Spokesperson, Unfreezing Assets to Meet the Critical Humanitarian Needs of the Libyan People, Washington, DC, August 25, 2011.

[20] European Council, EU implements latest U.N. decisions in support of Libya, September 22, 2011.

[21] The oil terminal at Brega reportedly suffered the most damage, along with support infrastructure elsewhere.

[22] Office of Foreign Assets Control, Statement of Licensing Policy on the Trade in Oil, Gas, and Petroleum Products Exported Under the Auspices of the Transitional National Council of Libya," (updated April 26, 2011), available at http://www.treasury.gov/resource-center/sanctions

[23] In May, U.N. Under-Secretary-General and Emergency Relief Coordinator Valerie Amos reported that "The manner in which the sanctions are implemented and monitored is causing serious delays in the arrival of commercial goods." U.N. Document S/PV.6530, Provisional Record of the 6530th meeting of the Security Council, May 9, 2011.

[24] Jehani remarks at United States Institute of Peace, September 23, 2011.

[25] Response to the Libyan Crisis, External Situation Report, September 7, 2011.

[26] For more information on the ICC and Africa, see CRS Report R41116, *The International Criminal Court (ICC): Jurisdiction, Extradition, and U.S. Policy*, by Emily C. Barbour and Matthew C. Weed and CRS Report RL34665, *International Criminal Court Cases in Africa: Status and Policy Issues*, coordinated by Alexis Arieff.

[27] ICC Prosecutor's Office, Public Redacted Version of Prosecutor's Application Pursuant to Article 58 as to Muammar Mohammed Abu Minyar Gaddafi, Saif Al-Islam Gaddafi, and Abdullah Al Senussi," May 16, 2011.

[28] U.N. Document S/PV.6528, Provisional Record of the 6528th meeting of the Security Council, May 4, 2011.

[29] For example, see International Crisis Group, "Popular Protest in North Africa and the Middle East (V): Making Sense of Libya," Middle East/North Africa Report No. 107, June 6, 2011.

[30] The commission members are Cherif Bassiouni of Egypt, Asma Khader of Jordan, and Philippe Kirsch of Canada. See U.N. Document A/HRC/17/44, "Report of the International

Commission of Inquiry to investigate all alleged violations of international human rights law in the Libyan Arab Jamahiriya," June 1, 2011.

[31] CRS obtained a draft interim national charter from an independent source as well as from a translated version available from the U.S. Open Source Center. Pending the availability of a final official version, this analysis is subject to change.

[32] OSC Report GMP20100128950040, "Libyan Minister of Justice Resigns Over 'Harsh' Criticism in People's Congress," January 28, 2010.

[33] Kareem Fahim, "Rebel Leadership Shows Signs of Strain in Libya," *New York Times*, April 4, 2011; Kim Sengupta, "Divided and Disorganised, Libyan Rebel Military Turn on NATO Allies," *The Independent* (UK), April 7, 2011; and, Rod Nordland, "As British Help Libyan Rebels, Aid Goes to a Divided Force," *New York Times*, April 19, 2011.

[34] One early April account described the opposition forces as follows: "The hard core of the fighters has been the *shabaab*—the young people whose protests in mid-February sparked the uprising. They range from street toughs to university students (many in computer science, engineering, or medicine), and have been joined by unemployed hipsters and middle-aged mechanics, merchants, and storekeepers. There is a contingent of workers for foreign companies: oil and maritime engineers, construction supervisors, translators. There are former soldiers, their gunstocks painted red, green, and black—the suddenly ubiquitous colors of the pre-Qaddafi Libyan flag. And there are a few bearded religious men, more disciplined than the others, who appear intent on fighting at the dangerous tip of the advancing lines.... With professional training and leadership (presumably from abroad), the rebels may eventually turn into something like a proper army. But, for now, they have perhaps only a thousand trained fighters, and are woefully outgunned." Jon Lee Anderson, "Who are the Rebels?" *The New Yorker*, April 4, 2011.

[35] OSC Report GMP20111020631002, "Libyan Defense Minister Makes Statement on Al-Qadhafi's Demise," October 20, 2011.

[36] Chris Adams, "Libyan rebel leader spent much of past 20 years in suburban Virginia," *McClatchy Newspapers*, March 26, 2011.

[37] OSC Report FTS19960821000373, "U.S.-Based Oppositionist Has 'Secret Meetings' Near Tripoli," August 21, 1996.

[38] Rod Nordland, "As British Help Libyan Rebels, Aid Goes to a Divided Force," *New York Times*, April 19, 2011.

[39] OSC Report GMP20110928120003, "Tripoli Rebel Leader on Security Situation, Differences With TNC, Others," September 28, 2011.

[40] May Youssef, "Anti-Gaddafists Rally in London," *Al Ahram Weekly (Cairo)*, No. 749, June 30 - July 6, 2005; *Al Jazeera (Doha)*, "Opposition Plans to Oust Al Qadhafi," June 25, 2005; *Middle East Mirror*, "Libya's Fractured Opposition," July 29, 2005.

[41] "Libyan Opposition Groups Meet in London To Reiterate Commitment To Save Libya," OSC Report GMP20080329825012, March 29, 2008.

[42] His family name also is transliterated as Al Senussi. Immediately prior to his departure for medical treatment in August 1969, the late King Idris signaled his intent to abdicate and pass authority to his crown prince and nephew, Hasan al Rida al Mahdi al Sanusi. Crown Prince Hasan was serving as regent during the Qadhafi coup, and he and his family were imprisoned and placed under house arrest until being allowed to leave Libya in the late 1980s. Each of King Idris's potential direct heirs died as children. Upon Prince Hasan's death in 1992, he passed the title of head of the Al Sanusi royal house to his son, Prince Mohammed al Rida al Sanusi.

[43] OSC Report GMP20110228405001, "Libyan Muslim Brotherhood Group Supports 'Glorious Revolution,'" February 28, 2011.

[44] Al Salabi is referred to in regional press outlets as a prominent Muslim Brotherhood supporter. In the past, Al Salabi facilitated the government's dialogue with imprisoned Islamists.

[45] In 2007, Abdel Qadir responded to political reform statements by Sayf al Islam al Qadhafi with calls for more inclusive, consultative decision making. In a November 2008 interview, Abdel Qadir noted that reform outreach was taking place under the auspices of the Qadhafi Foundation and not through official state organs, which in his view undermined the significance of the outreach. He also repeated calls for reform and reconciliation aimed at creating a constitution and protecting civil rights for Libyans. See OSC Report GMP20050803550006, "Al Jazirah TV Interviews Libyan Muslim Brotherhood Leader on Current Situation," August 3, 2005; OSC Report GMP20070830282001, "Libyan MB Concerned Over Sayf al-Islam's Statements Regarding New Constitution," August 30, 2007; and, OSC Report GMP20081111635001, "Libyan Muslim Brotherhood Official on Libya's Foreign, Domestic Politics," November 10, 2008.

[46] OSC Report GMP20110920825008, "Libya's MB Leader: Competence, Election Criteria for Government Formation," September 20, 2011.

[47] The two were group leaders Dr. Abdullah Ahmed Izzadin and Dr. Salem Mohammed Abu Hanek.

[48] Afaf El Geblawi, "Libya Frees All Jailed Muslim Brotherhood Members," *Agence France Presse*, March 3, 2006.

[49] The United States froze the LIFG's U.S. assets under Executive Order 13224 in September 2001, and formally designated the LIFG as a Foreign Terrorist Organization in December 2004.

[50] See U.S. Department of State, "Terrorist Organizations: LIFG," *Country Reports on Terrorism 2010*, August 2011.

[51] OSC Report FEA20071104393586, "Al-Zawahiri, Al-Libi: Libyan Islamic Fighting Group Joins Al-Qa'ida," November 3, 2007.

[52] OSC Report GMP20090703825003, "Libyan Islamic Fighting Group Abroad Issues Statement Supporting Regime Dialogue," July 3, 2009.

[53] Through this process, over 200 LIFG members were released from jail, including senior leaders and former commanders who have been active during the recent unrest. Prominent prisoners released under the auspices of the reconciliation program include former LIFG leader Abdelhakim Belhajj, former military director Khaled Sharif, and leading LIFG ideologue Sami Sa'idi. OSC Report GMP20100323950045, "Three leaders of Libyan Fighting Group freed – paper," March 23, 2010.

[54] OSC Report GMP20110217825017, "Libya: IFG Elements Establish New Group Aiming for Peaceful Regime Change," February 17, 2011.

[55] U.S. Department of the Treasury, "Treasury Designates UK-Based Individuals, Entities Financing Al QaidaAffiliated LIFG," JS-4016, February 8, 2006.

[56] U.S. Department of the Treasury, "Three LIFG Members Designation for Terrorism," HP-1244, October 30, 2008.

[57] Alison Pargeter, "Militant Groups Pose Security Challenge for Libyan Regime," *Janes Intelligence Review*, Vol. 17, No. 8, August 2005, pp. 16-19.

[58] OSC Report FEA20071104393586, "Al-Zawahiri, Al-Libi: Libyan Islamic Fighting Group Joins Al-Qa'ida," November 3, 2007.

[59] In a July 2009 statement, LIFG members in Britain characterized the November 2007 Al Qaeda affiliation announcement from the late Abu Layth Al Libi as "a personal decision

that is at variance with the basic status of the group," and sought to "clearly emphasize that the group is not, has never been, and will never be, linked to the Al Qaeda organization." OSC Report GMP20090703825003, "Libyan Islamic Fighting Group Abroad Issues Statement Supporting Regime Dialogue," July 3, 2009.

[60] "Report on 'Seething Anger' in Libya Over Dismantling Al Qa'ida-Linked Cells," OSC Report GMP20080630825001 June 30, 2008; "Libya: Jailed Islamic Group Leaders 'Preparing' To Renounce Armed Violence," OSC Report GMP20080706837002, July 6, 2008; "Libyan Islamic Fighting Group Source Announces Ideology Revision Nearly Complete," OSC Report GMP20090615825012, June 15, 2009; and OSC Reports, GMP20090911452001, GMP20090911452002, GMP2009091145200, GMP20090910488004, GMP200909 11452004, GMP20090915452001, "Libyan Newspaper Publishes Libyan Fighting Group Retractions," September 2009.

[61] OSC Report GMP20110313479001, "New Abu-Yahya al-Libi Video: 'To Our People in Libya,'" March 12, 2011.

[62] For more information on AQIM and its relationship to Al Qaeda, see CRS Report R41070, *Al Qaeda and Affiliates: Historical Perspective, Global Presence, and Implications for U.S. Policy*, coordinated by John Rollins.

[63] Kevin Peraino, "Destination Martyrdom," *Newsweek*, April 19, 2008. Al Hasadi claims to have recruited Libyans to fight in Iraq, but has publicly denied accusations he is affiliated with Al Qaeda or is seeking to establish Islamist rule in Darnah or on a national basis. Al Hasadi appeared on Al Jazeera and read a statement denying the Libyan government's accusations. See OSC Report GMP20110225648002, "Libya: Former LIFG Leader Denies Plan To Establish 'Islamic Emirate' in Darnah," February 25, 2011; and, OSC Report EUP20110322025008, "Libya: Rebel Leader in Derna Denies Local Presence of Extremists, Al-Qa'ida," March 22, 2011.

[64] See OSC Report GMP20110416825001, "Al-Qa'ida in Islamic Maghreb Spokesman Says There Are Islamic Amirates in Libya," April 16, 2011; and, OSC Report AFP20110418950070, "AQIM accuses Al-Hayat newspaper of falsifying interview with spokesman," April 18, 2011.

[65] Droukdel said "the battle you are fighting now with the tyrant ... It is itself the battle we fought yesterday and are fighting today." See OSC Report GMP20110318405002, "AQIM Amir's Audio Message to Libya, 'The Descendants of Umar al-Mukhtar,'" March 17, 2011.

[66] OSC Report FEA20110913021928, "Libya: TNC Chairman Says Sharia'h Law To Be Main Source of Legislation - Libya TV," September 12, 2011.

[67] OSC Report GMP20110822676001, "Libya's Abd-al-Jalil Warns of 'Extremist Islamists,' Threatens To Resign," August 22, 2011.

[68] OSC Report GMP20110828648003, "Libya: Rebel Military Commander Says No Al-Qa'ida Groups in Libya," August 28, 2011.

In: Libya
Editors: B. L. Kerr and M. I. Cantu ISBN: 978-1-61942-615-3

Chapter 3

REMARKS BY THE PRESIDENT ON THE DEATH OF MUAMMAR QADDAFI*

The White House
Office of the Press Secretary
October 20, 2011

THE PRESIDENT: Good afternoon, everybody. Today, the government of Libya announced the death of Muammar Qaddafi. This marks the end of a long and painful chapter for the people of Libya, who now have the opportunity to determine their own destiny in a new and democratic Libya.

For four decades, the Qaddafi regime ruled the Libyan people with an iron fist. Basic human rights were denied. Innocent civilians were detained, beaten and killed. And Libya's wealth was squandered. The enormous potential of the Libyan people was held back, and terror was used as a political weapon.

Today, we can definitively say that the Qaddafi regime has come to an end. The last major regime strongholds have fallen. The new government is consolidating the control over the country. And one of the world's longest-serving dictators is no more.

One year ago, the notion of a free Libya seemed impossible. But then the Libyan people rose up and demanded their rights. And when Qaddafi and his forces started going city to city, town by town, to brutalize men, women and children, the world refused to stand idly by.

---

* This is an edited, reformatted and augmented version of The White House, Office of the Press Secretary publication, dated October 20, 2011.

Faced with the potential of mass atrocities -- and a call for help from the Libyan people -- the United States and our friends and allies stopped Qaddafi's forces in their tracks. A coalition that included the United States, NATO and Arab nations persevered through the summer to protect Libyan civilians. And meanwhile, the courageous Libyan people fought for their own future and broke the back of the regime.

So this is a momentous day in the history of Libya. The dark shadow of tyranny has been lifted. And with this enormous promise, the Libyan people now have a great responsibility -- to build an inclusive and tolerant and democratic Libya that stands as the ultimate rebuke to Qaddafi's dictatorship. We look forward to the announcement of the country's liberation, the quick formation of an interim government, and a stable transition to Libya's first free and fair elections. And we call on our Libyan friends to continue to work with the international community to secure dangerous materials, and to respect the human rights of all Libyans — including those who have been detained.

We're under no illusions -- Libya will travel a long and winding road to full democracy. There will be difficult days ahead. But the United States, together with the international community, is committed to the Libyan people. You have won your revolution. And now, we will be a partner as you forge a future that provides dignity, freedom and opportunity.

For the region, today's events prove once more that the rule of an iron fist inevitably comes to an end. Across the Arab world, citizens have stood up to claim their rights. Youth are delivering a powerful rebuke to dictatorship. And those leaders who try to deny their human dignity will not succeed.

For us here in the United States, we are reminded today of all those Americans that we lost at the hands of Qaddafi's terror. Their families and friends are in our thoughts and in our prayers. We recall their bright smiles, their extraordinary lives, and their tragic deaths. We know that nothing can close the wound of their loss, but we stand together as one nation by their side.

For nearly eight months, many Americans have provided extraordinary service in support of our efforts to protect the Libyan people, and to provide them with a chance to determine their own destiny. Our skilled diplomats have helped to lead an unprecedented global response. Our brave pilots have flown in Libya's skies, our sailors have provided support off Libya's shores, and our leadership at NATO has helped guide our coalition. Without putting a single U.S. service member on the ground, we achieved our objectives, and our NATO mission will soon come to an end.

This comes at a time when we see the strength of American leadership across the world. We've taken out al Qaeda leaders, and we've put them on the path to defeat. We're winding down the war in Iraq and have begun a transition in Afghanistan. And now, working in Libya with friends and allies, we've demonstrated what collective action can achieve in the 21st century.

Of course, above all, today belongs to the people of Libya. This is a moment for them to remember all those who suffered and were lost under Qaddafi, and look forward to the promise of a new day. And I know the American people wish the people of Libya the very best in what will be a challenging but hopeful days, weeks, months and years ahead.

Thank you, very much.

In: Libya
Editors: B. L. Kerr and M. I. Cantu
ISBN: 978-1-61942-615-3

Chapter 4

LIBYA PROFILE*

United States Department of State

IMPORTANT NOTE

This State Department Profile was developed prior to the end of the Qadhafi regime on October 20, 2011. Nonetheless, it contains important background and historical information).

PROFILE

Geography

Location: North Africa, bordering the Mediterranean Sea, between Egypt, Tunisia, and Algeria, southern border with Chad, Niger, and Sudan.
Area: 1,759,540 sq. km.
Cities: Tripoli (capital), Benghazi.
Terrain: Mostly barren, flat to undulating plains, plateaus, depressions.
Climate: Mediterranean along coast; dry, extreme desert interior.
Land use: *Arable land*--1.03%; *permanent crops*--0.19%; *other*--98.78%.

---

* This is an edited, reformatted and augmented version of the United States Department of State publication, from http://www.state, dated July 2011.

People

Nationality: *Noun and adjective*--Libyan(s).
Population (July 2010 est.): 6,461,454.
Annual population growth rate (2010 est.): 2.117%.
Birth rate (2010 est.)--24.58 births/1,000 population.
Death rate (2010 est.)--3.45 deaths/1,000 population.
Ethnic groups: Berber and Arab 97%; other 3%
(includes Greeks, Maltese, Italians, Egyptians, Pakistanis, Turks, Indians, and Tunisians).
Religion: Sunni Muslim 97%, other 3%.
Languages: Arabic is the primary language.
English and Italian are understood in major cities.
Education: *Years compulsory*--9. *Attendance*--90%.
Literacy (age 15 and over who can read and write)—
total population 82.6%; male 92.4%; female 72% (2003 est.).

Health (2010 est.): *Infant mortality rate*--20.87 deaths/1,000 live births. *Life expectancy*--total population 77.47 yrs.; male 75.18 yrs.; female 79.88 yrs.
Work force (2010 est.): 1.686 million.

Government

(note: these details were in effect only prior to October 20, 2011).

Official name: Great Socialist People's Libyan Arab Jamahiriya.
Type: "Jamahiriya" is a term Col. Mu'ammar al-Qadhafi coined and which he defines as a "state of the masses" governed by the populace through local councils. In practice, Libya is an authoritarian state.
Independence: Libya declared independence on December 24, 1951.
Revolution Day: September 1, 1969.
Constitution: No formal document. Revolutionary edicts establishing a government structure were issued on December 11, 1969 and amended March 2, 1977 to establish popular congresses and people's committees that constitute the Jamahiriya system.
Administrative divisions: 32 municipalities (singular--"shabiya", plural--"shabiyat"): Butnan, Darnah, Gubba, al-Jebal al-Akhdar, Marj, al-Jebal al-Hezam, Benghazi, Ajdabiya, Wahat, Kufra, Surt, Al Jufrah, Misurata, Murgub, Bani-Walid, Tarhuna and Msallata, Tripoli, Jfara, Zawiya, Sabratha and Surman, An Nuqat al-Khams, Gharyan, Mezda, Nalut, Ghadames, Yefren, Wadi Alhaya, Ghat, Sabha, Wadi Shati, Murzuq, Tajura and an-Nuwaha al-Arba'a.
Political system: Political parties are banned. According to the political theory of Col. Mu'ammar al-Qadhafi, multi-layered popular assemblies (people's congresses) with executive institutions (people's committees) are guided by political cadres (revolutionary committees).
Suffrage: 18 years of age; universal and compulsory.

Economy

Real GDP (2009 est.): $85.04 billion.
GDP per capita (PPP, 2009 est.): $13,400.
Real GDP growth rate (2009 est.): -0.7%.

Natural resources: Petroleum, natural gas, gypsum.

Agriculture: *Products*--wheat, barley, olives, dates, citrus, vegetables, peanuts, soybeans; cattle; approximately 75% of Libya's food is imported.

Industry: *Types*--petroleum, food processing, textiles, handicrafts, cement.

Trade: *Exports* (2009 est.)--$34.24 billion: crude oil, refined petroleum products, natural gas, chemicals. *Major markets* (2009 est.)--Italy (37.65%), Germany (10.11%), Spain (7.94%), France (8.44%), Switzerland (5.93%), U.S. (5.27%). *Imports* (2009 est.)--$22.11 billion: machinery, transport equipment, food, manufactured goods, consumer products, semi-finished goods. *Major suppliers* (2009)--Italy (18.9%), China (10.54%), Turkey (9.92%), Germany (9.78%), Tunisia (5.25%), South Korea (4.02%).

PEOPLE

Libya has a small population in a large land area. Population density is about 50 persons per sq. km. (80/sq. mi.) in the two northern regions of Tripolitania and Cyrenaica, but falls to less than one person per sq. km. (1.6/sq. mi.) elsewhere. Ninety percent of the people live in less than 10% of the area, primarily along the coast. More than half the population is urban, mostly concentrated in the two largest cities, Tripoli and Benghazi. Thirty-three percent of the population is estimated to be under age 15.

Native Libyans are primarily a mixture of Arabs and Berbers. Small Tebou and Tuareg tribal groups in southern Libya are nomadic or semi-nomadic. Among foreign residents, the largest groups are citizens of other African nations, including North Africans (primarily Egyptians and Tunisians), West Africans, and other Sub-Saharan Africans.

HISTORY

For most of their history, the peoples of Libya have been subjected to varying degrees of foreign control. The Phoenicians, Carthaginians, Greeks, Romans, Vandals, and Byzantines ruled all or parts of Libya. Although the Greeks and Romans left impressive ruins at Cyrene, Leptis Magna, and Sabratha, little else remains today to testify to the presence of these ancient cultures.

The Arabs conquered Libya in the seventh century A.D. In the following centuries, most of the indigenous peoples adopted Islam and the Arabic language and culture. The Ottoman Turks conquered the country in the mid-16th century. Libya remained part of their empire, although at times virtually autonomous, until Italy invaded in 1911 and, in the face of years of resistance, made Libya a colony.

In 1934, Italy adopted the name "Libya" (used by the Greeks for all of North Africa, except Egypt) as the official name of the colony, which consisted of the Provinces of Cyrenaica, Tripolitania, and Fezzan. King Idris I, Emir of Cyrenaica, led Libyan resistance to Italian occupation between the two world wars. Allied forces removed Axis powers from Libya in February 1943. Tripolitania and Cyrenaica came under separate British administration, while the French controlled Fezzan. In 1944, Idris returned from exile in Cairo but declined to resume permanent residence in Cyrenaica until the removal in 1947 of some aspects of foreign control. Under the terms of the 1947 peace treaty with the Allies, Italy relinquished all claims to Libya.

On November 21, 1949, the UN General Assembly passed a resolution stating that Libya should become independent before January 1, 1952. King Idris I represented Libya in the subsequent UN negotiations. When Libya declared its independence on December 24, 1951, it was the first country to achieve independence through the United Nations and one of the first former European possessions in Africa to gain independence. Libya was proclaimed a constitutional and a hereditary monarchy under King Idris.

The discovery of significant oil reserves in 1959 and the subsequent income from petroleum sales enabled what had been one of the world's poorest countries to become extremely wealthy, as measured by per capita GDP. Although oil drastically improved Libya's finances, popular resentment grew as wealth was increasingly concentrated in the hands of the elite. This discontent continued to mount with the rise throughout the Arab world of Nasserism and the idea of Arab unity.

On September 1, 1969, a small group of military officers led by then 28-year-old army officer Mu'ammar Abu Minyar al-Qadhafi staged a coup d'etat against King Idris, who was subsequently exiled to Egypt. The new regime, headed by the Revolutionary Command Council (RCC), abolished the monarchy and proclaimed the new Libyan Arab Republic. Qadhafi emerged as leader of the RCC and eventually as de facto head of state, a political role he still plays. The Libyan Government asserts that Qadhafi currently holds no official position, although he is referred to in government statements and the official press as the "Brother Leader and Guide of the Revolution," among other honorifics.

The new RCC's motto became "freedom, socialism, and unity." It pledged itself to remedy "backwardness," take an active role in the Palestinian cause, promote Arab unity, and encourage domestic policies based on social justice, non-exploitation, and an equitable distribution of wealth.

An early objective of the new government was withdrawal of all foreign military installations from Libya. Following negotiations, British military installations at Tobruk and nearby El Adem were closed in March 1970, and U.S. facilities at Wheelus Air Force Base near Tripoli were closed in June 1970. That July, the Libyan Government ordered the expulsion of several thousand Italian residents. By 1971, libraries and cultural centers operated by foreign governments were ordered closed.

In the 1970s, Libya claimed leadership of Arab and African revolutionary forces and sought active roles in international organizations. Late in the 1970s, Libyan embassies were re-designated as "people's bureaus," as Qadhafi sought to portray Libyan foreign policy as an expression of the popular will. The people's bureaus, aided by Libyan religious, political, educational, and business institutions overseas, attempted to export Qadhafi's revolutionary philosophy abroad.

Qadhafi's confrontational foreign policies and use of terrorism, as well as Libya's growing friendship with the U.S.S.R., led to increased tensions with the West in the 1980s. Following a terrorist bombing at a discotheque in West Berlin frequented by American military personnel, in 1986 the U.S. retaliated militarily against targets in Libya, and imposed broad unilateral economic sanctions.

After Libya was implicated in the 1988 bombing of Pan Am flight 103 over Lockerbie, Scotland, UN sanctions were imposed in 1992. UN Security Council resolutions (UNSCRs) passed in 1992 and 1993 obliged Libya to fulfill requirements related to the Pan Am 103 bombing before sanctions could be lifted. Qadhafi initially refused to comply with these requirements, leading to Libya's political and economic isolation for most of the 1990s.

In 1999, Libya fulfilled one of the UNSCR requirements by surrendering two Libyans who were suspected to have been involved with the bombing for trial before a Scottish court in the Netherlands. One of these suspects, Abdel Basset Ali Mohamed al-Megrahi, was found guilty; the other was acquitted. Al-Megrahi's conviction was upheld on appeal in 2002. On August 19, 2009, al-Megrahi was released from Scottish prison on compassionate grounds due to a terminal illness and returned to Libya. In August 2003, Libya fulfilled the remaining UNSCR requirements, including acceptance of responsibility for the actions of its officials and payment of appropriate compensation to the victims' families. UN sanctions were lifted on September 12, 2003. U.S. International Emergency Economic Powers Act (IEEPA)-based sanctions were lifted September 20, 2004.

On December 19, 2003, Libya publicly announced its intention to rid itself of weapons of mass destruction (WMD) and Missile Technology Control Regime (MTCR)-class missile programs. Subsequently, Libya cooperated with the U.S., the U.K., the International Atomic Energy Agency, and the Organization for the Prohibition of Chemical Weapons toward these objectives. Libya has also signed the IAEA Additional Protocol and has become a State Party to the Chemical Weapons Convention. These were important steps toward full diplomatic relations between the U.S. and Libya.

Nationwide political violence erupted in February 2011, following the Libyan Government's brutal suppression of popular protests against Libyan leader Mu'ammar al-Qadhafi. Opposition forces quickly seized control of Benghazi, Libya's second-largest city, as well as significant portions of eastern Libya and some areas in western Libya. Drawing from the local opposition councils which formed the backbone of the "February 17" revolution, the Libyan opposition announced the formation of a Transitional National Council (TNC) on February 27, 2011. The Council has stated its desire to remove Qadhafi from power and establish a unified, democratic, and free Libya that respects universal human rights principles.

Government and Political Conditions

(note: these details were in effect only prior to October 20, 2011).

Libya's political system is in theory based on the political philosophy in Qadhafi's Green Book, which combines socialist and Islamic theories and rejects parliamentary democracy and political parties. In reality, Qadhafi exercises near-total control over major government decisions. During the first 7 years following the revolution, the Revolutionary Command Council, which included Colonel Qadhafi and 12 fellow army officers, began a complete overhaul of Libya's political system, society, and economy. In 1973, Qadhafi announced the start of a "cultural revolution" in schools, businesses, industries, and public institutions to oversee administration of those organizations in the public interest. On March 2, 1977, Qadhafi convened a General People's

Congress (GPC) to proclaim the establishment of "people's power," change the country's name to the Socialist People's Libyan Arab Jamahiriya, and to vest, theoretically, primary authority in the GPC.

The GPC is the legislative forum that interacts with the General People's Committee, whose members are secretaries of Libyan ministries. It serves as the intermediary between the masses and the leadership and is composed of the secretariats of some 600 local "basic popular congresses." The GPC secretariat and the cabinet secretaries are appointed by the GPC secretary general and confirmed by the annual GPC congress. These cabinet secretaries are responsible for the routine operation of their ministries, but Qadhafi exercises real authority directly or through manipulation of the peoples and revolutionary committees.

Qadhafi remained the de facto head of state and secretary general of the GPC until 1980, when he gave up his office. Although he holds no formal office, Qadhafi exercises power with the assistance of a small group of trusted advisers, who include relatives from his home base in the Sirte region, which lies between the traditional commercial and political power centers in Benghazi and Tripoli.

In the 1980s, competition grew between the official Libyan Government, military hierarchies, and the revolutionary committees. An abortive coup attempt in May 1984, apparently mounted by Libyan exiles with internal support, led to a short-lived reign of terror in which thousands were imprisoned and interrogated. An unknown number were executed. Qadhafi used the revolutionary committees to search out alleged internal opponents following the coup attempt, thereby accelerating the rise of more radical elements inside the Libyan power hierarchy.

In 1988, faced with rising public dissatisfaction with shortages in consumer goods and setbacks in Libya's war with Chad, Qadhafi began to curb the power of the revolutionary committees and to institute some domestic reforms. The regime released many political prisoners and eased restrictions on foreign travel by Libyans. Private businesses were again permitted to operate.

In the late 1980s, Qadhafi began to pursue an anti-Islamic fundamentalist policy domestically, viewing fundamentalism as a potential rallying point for opponents of the regime. Qadhafi's security forces launched a pre-emptive strike at alleged coup plotters in the military and among the Warfallah tribe in October 1993. Widespread arrests and government reshufflings followed, accompanied by public "confessions" from regime opponents and allegations of torture and executions. The military, once Qadhafi's strongest supporters, became a potential threat in the 1990s. In 1993, following a failed coup attempt that implicated senior military officers, Qadhafi began to purge the military periodically, eliminating potential rivals and inserting his own loyal followers in their place.

Qadhafi's strategy of frequent re-balancing of roles and responsibilities of his lieutenants makes it difficult for outsiders to understand Libyan politics. Several key political figures hold overlapping portfolios, and switch roles in a country where personalities and relationships often play more important roles than official titles. While high-ranking officials may have official portfolios, it is not uncommon for supposed subordinates to report directly to Qadhafi on issues thought to be within the purview of other officials. Foreign Minister Abdulati al-Obeidi was appointed to his position in March 2011, following the defection of his predecessor, Musa Kusa. Prime Minister al-Baghdadi al-Mahmoudi oversees the day-to-day operation of the Libyan cabinet, and plays a key role in setting financial and regulatory affairs, as well as domestic policies. Qadhafi's sons play an important role in government circles. Qadhafi's second son, Saif al-Islam al-Qadhafi, was previously viewed as a reformer but has emerged as a strong defender of the regime following the outbreak of political violence. His Qadhafi International Charity and Development Foundation (QDF) had served as a platform to advocate for greater respect for human rights, civil society development, and political and economic reforms. The QDF also played a key role in brokering dialogue with former Libyan Islamic Fighting Group members (LIFG), which led to their subsequent release from prison, and recantation of violence as a tool of jihad. Qadhafi's younger sons, Khamis and Saadi, are commanding military units, while his fourth son, Mutassim, had served as National Security Adviser and continues to be involved in security and military relations.

The Libyan court system consists of three levels: the courts of first instance; the courts of appeals; and the Supreme Court, which is the final appellate level. The GPC appoints justices to the Supreme Court. Special "revolutionary courts" and military courts operate outside the court system to try political offenses and crimes against the state. "People's courts," another example of extrajudicial authority, were abolished in January 2005. Libya's justice system is nominally based on Shari'a law.

The Libyan Transitional National Council has set up a rival government in Benghazi. The 45-member Council includes representatives from throughout Libya and is headed by Chairman (and former Qadhafi Minister of Justice) Mustafa Abdul Jalil. The Council acts as the opposition's legislative branch and has appointed an executive committee, headed by Mahmoud Jibril, to oversee interim governance issues. The TNC has stated repeatedly its desire to serve only as an interim body and has issued plans to draft a constitution and hold nationwide elections as soon as Qadhafi is removed from power.

Principal Government Officials

(note: these details were in effect only prior to October 20, 2011).

De facto Head of State--Mu'ammar Abu Minyar al-Qadhafi ("the Brother Leader and Guide of the Revolution")

Secretary General of the General People's Committee (Prime Minister)--Al-Baghdadi Ali al-Mahmudi

Secretary of the General People's Committee for Foreign Liaison and International Cooperation (Foreign Minister)--Abdulati al-Obeidi

The Libyan People's Bureau (embassy-equivalent) is located at 2600 Virginia Avenue NW, Suite 705, Washington DC 20037 (tel. 202-944-9601, fax 202-944-9603). However, it suspended operations on March 16, 2011, at the behest of the U.S. State Department.

ECONOMY

The government dominates Libya's socialist-oriented economy through control of the country's oil resources, which account for approximately 95% of export earnings, 75% of government receipts, and 25% of gross domestic product. Oil production, previously constant at just below Libya's Organization of Petroleum Exporting Countries (OPEC) quota of 1.4 million barrels per day (bpd), ground to a halt following the outbreak of political violence in February 2011. Oil revenues constitute the principal source of foreign exchange. Much of the country's income over the years has been lost to waste, corruption, conventional armaments purchases, and attempts to develop weapons of mass destruction, as well as to large donations made to developing countries in attempts to increase Qadhafi's influence in Africa and elsewhere. Although oil revenues and a small population have given Libya one of the highest per capita GDPs in Africa, the government's mismanagement of the economy has led to high inflation and increased import prices. These factors resulted in a decline in the standard of living from the late 1990s through 2003, especially for lower and middle income strata of the Libyan society.

On September 20, 2004, President George W. Bush signed an Executive Order ending economic sanctions imposed under the authority of the International Emergency Economic Powers Act (IEEPA). Under the 2004 order, U.S. persons were no longer prohibited from working in Libya, and many American companies in diverse sectors actively sought investment opportunities in Libya. In 2008, the government announced ambitious plans to increase foreign investment in the oil and gas sectors to significantly boost production capacity from 1.2 million bpd to 3 million bpd by 2012, a target that the National Oil Corporation later estimated would to slip to 2017. In February 2011, the U.S. and UN imposed sanctions on Libya following the outbreak of political violence.

The government had been pursuing a number of large-scale infrastructure development projects such as highways, railways, air and seaports, telecommunications, water works, public housing, medical centers, shopping centers, and hotels. Despite efforts to diversify the economy and encourage private sector participation, extensive controls of prices, credit, trade, and foreign exchange have constrained growth. Import restrictions and inefficient resource allocations have caused periodic shortages of basic goods and foodstuffs, shortages that are worsening as the political unrest continues. Libya faces a long road ahead in liberalizing the socialist-oriented economy and recovering from the losses of the ongoing conflict, but initial steps, including applying for World Trade Organization (WTO) membership, reducing some subsidies, and announcing plans for privatization, have laid the groundwork for a transition to a more market-based economy. The non-oil manufacturing and construction sectors, which account for more than 20% of GDP, have expanded from processing mostly agricultural products to include the production of petrochemicals, iron, steel, and aluminum. Climatic conditions and poor soils severely limit agricultural output, and Libya imports about 75% of its food. Libya's primary agricultural water source remains the Great Manmade River Project, but significant resources have been invested in desalinization research to meet growing water demands. Government officials have also indicated interest in developing markets for alternative sources of energy, pharmaceuticals, health care services, and oil production byproducts.

FOREIGN RELATIONS

Since 1969, Qadhafi has determined Libya's foreign policy. His principal foreign policy goals have been Arab unity, the incorporation of Israel and the

Palestinian Territories into a single nation of "Isratine," advancement of Islam, support for Palestinians, elimination of outside, particularly Western, influence in the Middle East and Africa, and support for a range of "revolutionary" causes.

After the 1969 coup, Qadhafi closed American and British bases on Libyan territory and partially nationalized all foreign oil and commercial interests in Libya. He also played a key role in promoting the use of oil embargoes as a political weapon for challenging the West, hoping that an oil price rise and embargo in 1973 would persuade the West, especially the United States, to end support for Israel. Qadhafi rejected both Soviet communism and Western capitalism, and claimed he was charting a middle course.

Libya's relationship with the former Soviet Union involved massive Libyan arms purchases from the Soviet bloc and the presence of thousands of east bloc advisers. Libya's use, and heavy loss, of Soviet-supplied weaponry in its war with Chad was a notable breach of an apparent Soviet-Libyan understanding not to use the weapons for activities inconsistent with Soviet objectives. As a result, Soviet-Libyan relations reached a nadir in mid-1987.

After the fall of the Warsaw Pact and the Soviet Union, Libya concentrated on expanding diplomatic ties with Third World countries and increasing its commercial links with Europe and East Asia. These ties significantly diminished after the imposition of UN sanctions in 1992. Following a 1998 Arab League meeting in which fellow Arab states decided not to challenge UN sanctions, Qadhafi announced that he was turning his back on pan-Arab ideas, which had been one of the fundamental tenets of his philosophy.

Instead, over the last decade, Libya pursued closer bilateral ties with North African neighbors Egypt, Tunisia, and Morocco, and greater Africa. It has sought to develop its relations with Sub-Saharan Africa, leading to Libyan involvement in several internal African disputes in the Democratic Republic of the Congo, Sudan, Mauritania, Somalia, Central African Republic, Eritrea, and Ethiopia. Libya has also sought to expand its influence in Africa through financial assistance, granting aid donations to impoverished neighbors such as Niger and oil subsidies to Zimbabwe, and through participation in the African Union. Qadhafi has proposed a borderless "United States of Africa" to transform the continent into a single nation-state ruled by a single government. This plan has been greeted with skepticism. In recent years, Libya has played a helpful role in facilitating the provision of humanitarian assistance to Darfur refugees in Chad, contributing to efforts to forge a ceasefire between Chad and Sudan, and bringing an end to the conflict in Darfur.

One of the longest-standing issues in Libya's relationship with the European Union and the international community was resolved in July 2007 with the release of five Bulgarian nurses and a Palestinian doctor who had been convicted in 1999 of deliberately infecting over 400 children in a Benghazi hospital with the HIV virus. The six medics were sentenced to death in 2004, a sentence that was upheld by the Libyan Supreme Court, but commuted in July 2007 by the Higher Judicial Council to life in prison. Under a previous agreement with the Bulgarian Government on the repatriation of prisoners, the medics were allowed to return to Bulgaria to finish their sentence, where upon arrival the Bulgarian president pardoned all six. The Benghazi International Fund, established by the United States and its European allies, raised $460 million to distribute to the families of the children infected with HIV, each of whom received $1 million.

Following Libya's 2003 decision to dismantle its WMD programs and renounce terrorism, it sought to actively reengage the international community through improved bilateral relations with the West, as well as seeking leadership positions within international organizations. Libya served on the International Atomic Energy Agency's Board of Governors from 2007-2008. From 2008-2009, it served a 2-year non-permanent tenure on the UN Security Council representing the Africa group. In 2009, Libya became chair for 1 year of the African Union and played host to several AU summits. The same year, it assumed the UN General Assembly presidency. Libya took over the Arab League presidency in 2010 and hosted the March and October 2010 Arab League summits and an Arab-African summit in October 2010.

After 40 years in power, Qadhafi made his first trip to the United States in September 2009 to participate in the United Nations General Assembly (UNGA) in New York City and deliver his country's speech. Qadhafi's UNGA speech reinforced Libya's assimilation within the international community and its emerging importance on the African scene. The trip came on the heels of the release from Scotland and return to Libya of convicted Pan Am 103 bomber Abdel Basset Ali Mohamed al-Megrahi.

Libya's relations with the rest of the world deteriorated sharply following Qadhafi's brutal suppression of popular protests in February 2011. The UN quickly took action to try to end the violence, passing UNSCR 1970 on February 26, which called for a referral to the International Criminal Court, an arms embargo, a travel ban, an asset freeze, and sanctions. UNSCR 1973, adopted on March 17, authorized member states to take military action to protect civilians and civilian populated areas under threat of attack. Under the auspices of UNSCR 1973, the U.S., U.K., and France launched military action in Libya on March 20; NATO continued these efforts as "Operation Unified Protection."

Working through the international Contact Group on Libya, key members of the international community, including the U.S., have joined together to increase pressure on the Qadhafi regime and support the TNC. Several countries, including France, Italy, Qatar, and the U.K., have recognized the TNC as Libya's governing authority; countless others, including the U.S., have identified the TNC as the credible interlocutor of the Libyan people. More than 20 nations have diplomatic representation in Benghazi.

Terrorism

In 1999, the Libyan Government surrendered two Libyans suspected of involvement in the Pan Am 103 bombing, leading to the suspension of UN sanctions. On January 31, 2001, a Scottish court seated in the Netherlands found one of the suspects, Abdel Basset Ali al-Megrahi, guilty of murder in connection with the bombing, and acquitted the second suspect, Al-Amin Khalifa Fhima. Megrahi's conviction was upheld on March 14, 2002, but in October 2008 the Scottish High Court permitted Megrahi to appeal aspects of his case, formal hearings for which started in March 2009, when two separate requests for Megrahi's release where concurrently considered by Scottish Justice authorities: the first involved Libya's request for Megrahi's transfer under the U.K.-Libya Prisoner Transfer Agreement, and the other for his release on compassionate grounds. After a Scottish medical committee announced that Megrahi's life expectancy was less than 3 months (thereby falling under compassionate release guidelines), Scottish Justice Minister Kenny MacAskill granted Megrahi's release from prison, and permitted him to return to Libya on August 20, 2009. The decision provoked widespread objections by the Lockerbie bombing victims' families, who were particularly enraged by what appeared to be a "hero's welcome" in Tripoli.

UN sanctions were lifted on September 12, 2003 following Libyan compliance with its remaining UNSCR requirements on Pan Am 103, including acceptance of responsibility for the actions of its officials and payment of appropriate compensation. Libya had paid compensation in 1999 for the death of British policewoman Yvonne Fletcher, a move that preceded the reopening of the British Embassy in Tripoli, and had paid damages to the non-U.S. families of the victims in the bombing of UTA Flight 772. With the lifting of UN sanctions in September 2003, each of the families of the victims of Pan Am 103 received $4 million of a maximum $10 million in compensation. After the lifting of U.S. IEEPA-based sanctions on September 20, 2004, the families received a further $4 million.

On November 13, 2001, a German court found four persons, including a former employee of the Libyan embassy in East Berlin, guilty in connection with the 1986 La Belle disco bombing, in which two U.S. servicemen were killed. The court also established a connection to the Libyan Government. The German Government demanded that Libya accept responsibility for the La Belle bombing and pay appropriate compensation. A compensation deal for non-U.S. victims was agreed to in August 2004.

By 2003, Libya appeared to have curtailed its support for international terrorism, although it may have retained residual contacts with some of its former terrorist clients. In an August 2003 letter to the UN Security Council, Libya took significant steps to mend its international image and formally renounced terrorism. In August 2004, the Department of Justice entered into a plea agreement with Abdulrahman Alamoudi, in which he stated that he had been part of a 2003 plot to assassinate Saudi Crown Prince Abdallah (now King Abdallah) at the behest of Libyan Government officials. In 2005, the Saudi Government pardoned the individuals accused in the assassination plot.

During the 2005 UN General Assembly session, Libyan Foreign Minister Abd al-Rahman Shalgam issued a statement that reaffirmed Libya's commitment to the statements made in its letter addressed to the Security Council on August 15, 2003, renouncing terrorism in all its forms and pledging that Libya would not support acts of international terrorism or other acts of violence targeting civilians, whatever their political views or positions. Libya also expressed its commitment to continue cooperating in the international fight against terrorism. On June 30, 2006, the U.S. rescinded Libya's designation as a state sponsor of terrorism.

In May 2008, the U.S. and Libya began negotiations on a comprehensive claims settlement agreement to resolve outstanding claims of American and Libyan nationals against each country in their respective courts. On August 4, 2008 President Bush signed into law the Libyan Claims Resolution Act, which Congress had passed on July 31. The act provided for the restoration of Libya's sovereign, diplomatic, and official immunities before U.S. courts if the Secretary of State certified that the United States Government had received sufficient funds to resolve outstanding terrorism-related death and physical injury claims against Libya. Subsequently, both sides signed a comprehensive claims settlement agreement on August 14. On October 31, Secretary of State Condoleezza Rice certified to Congress that the United States had received $1.5 billion pursuant to the U.S.-Libya Claims Settlement Agreement. These funds were sufficient to provide the required compensation to victims of terrorism under the Libyan Claims Resolution Act. Concurrently, President Bush issued an executive order to implement the claims settlement agreement.

In September 2009, several leading members of the Libyan Islamic Fighting Group (LIFG) released a more than 400-page document in which they renounced violence and laid out what they claimed to be a clearer understanding of the ethics of Islamic Shari'a law and jihad, parting ways with Al-Qaeda and other terrorist groups whose violent methods they described as ignorant and illegitimate. The release of this revisionist manuscript shortly followed a public statement in August 2009, in which LIFG's leaders apologized to the Libyan leader for their violent acts and pledged to continue working toward a complete reconciliation with remaining elements of LIFG in Libya or abroad. LIFG's revised ideology and the subsequent release of many of its imprisoned members was due in large part to a 2-year initiative by Saif al-Islam al-Qadhafi, in his capacity as Chairman of the Qadhafi International Charity and Development Foundation, to broker the reconciliation between the Libyan Government and elements of LIFG leadership.

U.S.-Libyan Relations

The United States supported the UN resolution providing for Libyan independence in 1951 and raised the status of its office in Tripoli from a consulate general to a legation. Libya opened a legation in Washington, DC in 1954. Both countries subsequently raised their missions to embassy level.

After Qadhafi's 1969 coup, U.S.-Libyan relations became increasingly strained because of Libya's foreign policies supporting international terrorism and subversion against moderate Arab and African governments. In 1972, the United States withdrew its ambassador. Export controls on military equipment and civil aircraft were imposed during the 1970s, and U.S. embassy staff members were withdrawn from Tripoli after a mob attacked and set fire to the embassy in December 1979. The U.S. Government designated Libya a "state sponsor of terrorism" on December 29, 1979. In May 1981, the U.S. Government closed the Libyan "people's bureau" (embassy) in Washington, DC, and expelled the Libyan staff in response to a general pattern of conduct by the people's bureau contrary to internationally accepted standards of diplomatic behavior.

In August 1981, two Libyan jets fired on U.S. aircraft participating in a routine naval exercise over international waters of the Mediterranean claimed by Libya. The U.S. planes returned fire and shot down the attacking Libyan aircraft. In December 1981, the State Department invalidated U.S. passports for travel to Libya and, for purposes of safety, advised all U.S. citizens in Libya to leave. In March 1982, the U.S. Government prohibited imports of Libyan crude oil into the United States and expanded the controls on U.S.-origin goods intended for export to Libya. Licenses were required for all transactions, except food and medicine. In March 1984, U.S. export controls were expanded to prohibit future exports to the Ras Lanuf petrochemical complex. In April 1985, all Export-Import Bank financing was prohibited.

Due to Libya's continuing support for terrorism, the United States adopted additional economic sanctions against Libya in January 1986, including a total ban on direct import and export trade, commercial contracts, and travel-related activities. In addition, Libyan Government assets in the United States were frozen. When evidence of Libyan complicity was discovered in the Berlin discotheque terrorist bombing that killed two American servicemen, the United States responded by launching an aerial bombing attack against targets near Tripoli and Benghazi in April 1986. Subsequently, the United States maintained its trade and travel embargoes and brought diplomatic and economic pressure to bear against Libya. This pressure helped to bring about the 2003 Lockerbie settlement and Libya's renunciation of WMD and MTCR-class missiles.

In 1991, two Libyan intelligence agents were indicted by federal prosecutors in the U.S. and Scotland for their involvement in the December 1988 bombing of Pan Am flight 103. In January 1992, the UN Security Council approved Resolution 731 demanding that Libya surrender the suspects, cooperate with the Pan Am 103 and UTA 772 investigations, pay compensation to the victims' families, and cease all support for terrorism. Libya's refusal to comply led to the approval of UNSC Resolution 748 on March 31, 1992, imposing sanctions designed to bring about Libyan compliance. Continued Libyan defiance led to passage of UNSC Resolution 883, a limited assets freeze and an embargo on selected oil equipment, in November 1993. UN sanctions were lifted on September 12, 2003, after Libya fulfilled all remaining UNSCR requirements, including renunciation of terrorism, acceptance of responsibility for the actions of its officials, and payment of appropriate compensation to the victims' families.

On December 19, 2003, Libya announced its intention to rid itself of WMD and MTCR-class missile programs. Subsequently, it cooperated with the U.S., the U.K., the International Atomic Energy Agency, and the Organization for the Prohibition of Chemical Weapons toward these objectives. Libya has also signed the IAEA Additional Protocol and has become a State Party to the Chemical Weapons Convention.

In recognition of these actions, the U.S. began the process of normalizing relations with Libya. The U.S. terminated the applicability of the Iran-Libya Sanctions Act to Libya, and President Bush signed an Executive Order on September 20, 2004 terminating the national emergency with respect to Libya and ending IEEPA-based economic sanctions. This action had the effect of unblocking assets blocked under the Executive Order sanctions. Restrictions on cargo aviation and third-party code-sharing were lifted, as were restrictions on passenger aviation. Certain export controls remained in place.

U.S. diplomatic personnel reopened the U.S. Interest Section in Tripoli on February 8, 2004. The mission was upgraded to a U.S. Liaison Office on June 28, 2004, and to a full embassy on May 31, 2006. The establishment in 2005 of an American School in Tripoli demonstrated the increased presence of Americans in Libya and the normalization of bilateral relations. Libya re-established its diplomatic presence in Washington with the opening of an Interest Section on July 8, 2004, which was subsequently upgraded to a Liaison Office in December 2004 and to a full embassy on May 31, 2006.

On May 15, 2006, the State Department announced its intention to rescind Libya's designation as a state sponsor of terrorism in recognition of the fact that Libya had met the statutory requirements for such a move: it had not provided any support for acts of international terrorism in the preceding 6-month period, and had provided assurances that it would not do so in the future. On June 30, 2006, the U.S. rescinded Libya's designation as a state sponsor of terrorism.

In 2007, there were a series of senior-level meetings between U.S. and Libyan officials that focused on a broad array of issues, including regional security and counterterrorism cooperation. Secretary Rice, in her meeting with Foreign Minister Shalgam on the margins of the UN General Assembly, discussed the resolution of outstanding issues and charting a path for future cooperation. On July 11, President Bush nominated career diplomat Gene A. Cretz as U.S. Ambassador to Libya.

On January 3, 2008, Foreign Minister Shalgam made an official visit to Washington, the first official visit by a Libyan Foreign Minister since 1972. During that visit the United States and Libya signed a science and technology cooperation agreement, their first bilateral agreement since the downgrading of diplomatic relations.

In 2008, the U.S. and Libya concluded the U.S.-Libya Claims Settlement Agreement to resolve outstanding claims of American and Libyan nationals against each country in their respective courts. The same year, the Libyan Claims Resolution Act was signed into law by President Bush, providing for the restoration of Libya's sovereign, diplomatic, and official immunities before U.S. courts.

Resolution of outstanding claims permitted full normalization of ties and the exchange of ambassadors in January 2009 for the first time since 1973. U.S. Ambassador Gene A. Cretz was sworn in on December 17, 2008 and submitted his credentials to the General People's Committee on January 11, 2009. Libyan Ambassador Ali Suleiman Aujali submitted his credentials to President Bush on January 8, 2009. (He resigned on February 22, 2011 due to the Libyan Government's suppression of popular protests and became the TNC's representative to Washington.)

The normalization of relations provided the United States and Libya with increased opportunities to push for progress in areas of mutual concern, such as nonproliferation, counterterrorism, trade and investment, human rights, and economic development. On January 16, 2009, the U.S. and Libya signed a Defense Contacts and Cooperation Memorandum of Understanding. On April 21, 2009, National Security Adviser Mutassim al-Qadhafi visited Washington, DC and met with Secretary of State Hillary Clinton, as well as other senior U.S. Government officials. In September 2009, Qadhafi visited the U.S. for the first time to participate in the UN General Assembly in New York. In May 2010, the U.S. and Libya signed a Trade Investment Framework Agreement.

Relations with Libya deteriorated sharply following the Qadhafi regime's brutal suppression of popular protests. The U.S. suspended Embassy operations in Tripoli on February 25, 2011 and ordered the Libyan Government to suspend its Embassy operations in Washington on March 16. A mob overran and burned the U.S. Embassy on May 1. The U.S. imposed sanctions on Libya on February 25 and, in compliance with UNSCR 1970, froze more than $30 billion in Libyan Government assets. The U.S. appointed a special envoy to the Libyan opposition in March and has had a diplomatic presence in Benghazi since April 5, 2011.

INDEX

C

D

E

F

G

H

I

J

K

L

M

N

O

P

T

U

V

W

Z